THE HEART OF THE
EVANGELICAL FAITH

ISBN 0 7223 1501-5

Printed in Great Britain by
Arthur H. Stockwell Ltd.
Elms Court   Ilfracombe
Devon

Contents

Foreword

There are two ideas which we should definitely bypass — the first, that it does not matter what one believes, it is character and conduct that matter; and the second, that what matters so far as the Christian is concerned, is that he is doctrinally sound. The emphasis of the one is on conduct; and of the other, on creed.

The book here presented is not on conduct, but on belief. Its subject is not fruits, but roots; not effects, but causes; but these roots if they are living, will issue in fruits; these causes will produce effects.

The transcendence of Jesus Christ, and the uniqueness of Christianity, both taught in the inspired Word, need special emphasis today.

This latest production of the work of the late Pastor Robert Clarke is a worthy addition to his other writings: *The Uniqueness of the Church* (Stockwell Ltd.), *The Christ of God* (Victory Press), and *New Testament Christians* (Victory Press). While times change, God's Eternal Truth does not, and neither do men's hearts — a must for all who care deeply for Evangelical Truth.

Our prayer is that through the study of this book some may be enabled to see the truth concerning Christ and His Redeeming Work more clearly, and to love Him more dearly. It is sent forth with the prayer,

8

too, that God by His Spirit will bless it to the magnification of His Sovereign Grace, the glorification of His beloved Son, the edification of His redeemed people, and the salvation of precious souls.

Preface

No one can look at the world today with its divisions, its suffering, its inequalities, and its need without realizing that something, somewhere, has gone wrong. The condition of things in the world is not the directive will of God. In His sovereignty He permits certain things for the time being. He has His remedy for sin which is the root cause of all the trouble. He has a plan for the ages to come.

In the world there are many philosophies, many ideologies, and many plans for the betterment of mankind. Most of them are good enough but they fail, because they cannot change the heart of man. They cannot give new life, a new dynamic, and a new purpose. The heart of the problem is the problem of the heart. The Bible says: 'The heart is deceitful above all things, and desperately wicked: who can know it?' (Jer. 17:9).

Christianity has a message of pardon, of life, of power, of victory, and of hope. No one can deny that if this message were accepted and applied in the affairs of men things would be different. Centred in Christ, the God-man Redeemer and the Risen Lord, this message is unique. One feels that today some who claim to be Christians have got away from the heart of things.

We are against dogma, the theories of men, which are contrary to the truths of the Bible. But we stand for doctrine, the revelation of God in the Bible. Paul wrote to Titus saying: 'But speak thou the things which become sound doctrine' (Tit. 2:1). The inspired prediction is: 'For the time is coming when people will not endure sound teaching, but having itching ears they will accumulate for themselves teachers to suit their own likings, and will turn away from listening to the truth and wander into myths' (2 Tim. 4:3,4 R.S.V.). 'Now the Spirit expressly says that in the later times some will depart from the faith by giving heed to deceitful spirits and doctrines of demons' (1 Tim. 4:1 R.S.V.). The Bishop, the Elder, the Pastor of the local church must 'be able to give instruction in sound doctrine and also to confute those who contradict it' (Tit. 1:9 R.S.V.).

We cannot give up doctrines which transcend unenlightened human reason for the sake of simplicity or in the interests of ecclesiastical uniformity. Today people are compelled to believe certain things which they cannot fully understand or explain, things which a few years ago would have been rejected as incredible. Scientists are using the laws of nature, which are the laws of God, to accomplish what seemed impossible only a few years ago. God can use laws which are unknown to us, or He can use a new combination of known laws to accomplish His will.

If people want a religion that can be put into logical syllogisms or into neat theological definitions they had better not turn to New Testament Christianity. The truth of God is bigger than all our Creeds, bigger than all our Confessions of Faith, bigger than any Basis of

Doctrine. It may not be less than some of these, but it certainly is more than all of them put together. We cannot put the mighty ocean of Divine truth into the teacup of human conception and human definition.

To say: 'Live the life; do good, and never mind about doctrine' is to repudiate large portions of the Bible, for it is full of doctrine. Doctrine is basic to life and conduct. No builder will say: 'Never mind the foundation, go on with the building'. The divorcing of doctrine from conduct is not according to the will of God.

In this book there is doctrine, profound doctrine, which, we believe, is according to the Bible — the final court of appeal in all matters of faith and practice. We hope that the study of this book will lead to a deeper appreciation of God's truth and to holy, consistent, Christ-centred living.

Robert Clarke
3 Glentoye Park,
Newtownabbey,
Co. Antrim, N. Ireland

Chapter 1

THE TRUTH ABOUT GOD

The Gospel is the Gospel of God, that is, it is from God and about God. It is not man-originated or man-centred. Man hasn't broken through out of time into eternity to find out what God is like. God has come through from eternity into time to reveal Himself to man and to redeem man to Himself by the blood of the Cross. This is good news; this is glad tidings of great joy. Paul wrote about 'the glorious Gospel of the blessed God' which was committed to his trust (1 Tim. 1:11). The Gospel is a message from God and about God, about the glory, and grace, and greatness of Him who dwells in everlasting felicity. Man by searching has found out many wonderful things, but he could never have discovered the mysteries of the Incarnation, God made manifest in sinless humanity, or the mystery of the Atonement, God dealing with human sin and providing salvation full and free for the whosoever will.

The Sovereignty of God

There is the kingdom of God, which is either His rule or the realm over which He rules, probably both. There is the general rule of God which includes everyone and everything, even Satan and his hosts. God's kingdom ruleth over all. But there is a spiritual realm over which He rules by His Holy Spirit. This is entered only by the new birth. Our Lord said: 'Except a man be born again, he cannot see the kingdom of God' (John 3:3). Where the King is, there is the kingdom. We cannot be in saving relationship with the King without being in His kingdom. Believers in Christ are in the kingdom, for Paul says, 'God hath delivered us from the power of darkness, and hath translated us into the kingdom of his dear Son' (Col. 1:13).

Transcendence and immanence are both true. God is outside all and over all. He is also in all and through all. Dr A.H. Strong says that transcendence alone is God banished; immanence alone is God imprisoned. He is the author of natural laws, but He is not a prisoner in them. He is not so much 'up there' that He isn't 'down here', and He isn't so much 'down here' that He isn't 'up there'. Some may talk so much about the God of 'the depths' that they are almost pantheistic in philosophy.

The Bible teaches that God is on the throne, ruling over all and overruling all to His glory and to the good of those who trust in Him. This is good news. In the Old Testament we read: 'The Lord reigneth . . . . He sitteth between the cherubims' (Ps. 99:1). He sits enthroned upon the cherubim. The cherubim overshadowed the mercy seat which was sprinkled with the blood of atonement. The truth of the Bible is that God's sovereignty is never divorced from His mercy. God is not a whimsical, capricious dictator. There is the grace of Divine sovereignty as well as the sovereignty of Divine grace. Advocates of one system of theology may be inclined to forget this.

In the New Testament we read of 'the throne of God and of the Lamb' (Rev. 22:1). At the heart of God's sovereignty there is grace, all-sufficient grace, boundless grace, grace for all who really want it. It is sometimes said: 'God is sovereign and He can do as He pleases'. Yes, but we should remember that what He pleases is always just, and fair, and good. It is always in accordance with His own laws of justice. There are some things which God cannot do, some things which He chooses not to do. He cannot do anything that is unjust and unfair. Righteousness and justice are the habitation of His throne. There is no miscarriage of justice with God. In Psalm 145 there is a verse which is good news, pure gold. It says: 'The Lord is righteous in all His ways and gracious in all His works' (v.18). He doesn't do anything that outrages our sense of right and justice, for this sense is from Himself. God has been maligned and misrepresented so we need to proclaim the truth of the Bible concerning Him. The sovereignty of God is the sovereignty of a God of unerring wisdom and of unutterable love, not the rule of a whimsical dictator. We repudiate the idea that God sits in an ivory tower outside space, damning some people and saving others in a whimsical kind of way. He is on the throne of glory as a God of love and of justice. He is also inside time and space as a free personal Spirit; and He acts in a just and loving way.

The sovereignty of God is an overruling sovereignty. 'And we know that all things work together for good to them that love God, to them that are the called according to his purpose' (Rom. 8:28). Some manuscripts have God before 'work together'. This is the mind of the Spirit. It is not that all things work together in a mechanical, haphazard way. God works all things, the bitter and the sweet, the sad and the joyful, into a pattern for good to them who love Him and who do His will. If we don't love Him, obey Him, and serve Him, we cannot claim the truth of Romans 8:28.

'For things that seemed not good, yet turned to good, we thank Thee, Lord' (John Oxenham).

Christ came and lived, and suffered, and died. The question has been asked: 'Where was God when Christ was crucified?' The answer is: 'He was there suffering with Christ and for the world'. After Calvary there was the resurrection morning. 'Earth's saddest day and gladdest day were only one day apart'. One was going to say that every Calvary has its resurrection morning, but then one remembers there was only one Calvary — the Calvary of unparalleled suffering, and the Calvary of atoning Sacrifice. One can say that every night of suffering for God is followed by the morning of reward by God. It seems a long time before the sun rises, but rise it shall in shining splendour. There is yet to be a morning without clouds, without the clouds of sin, of doubt, of fear, of suffering, of misunderstanding of inequality, of mystery, and of need of any kind.

The sovereignty of God deals with man as a free, moral personality, not as a machine. God made man with personality, self-consciousness, self-determination, and the powers of choice. So there is the *permissive will* of God as well as the *directive* will of God. He allowed Hitler to put to death six million Jews, but He didn't cause him to do it. Dr A.T. Robertson says: 'Paul accepts fully human free agency but behind it all and through it all runs God's sovereignty and on its gracious side (2 Tim. 1:9)'. E.K. Simpson says: 'It is not for us to reconcile the antinomy between divine sovereignty and human free agency. That abyss mocks our sounding-lines'. We may be sure of this: No man is driven to eternal destruction by forces over which he has no control. No man is damned by God without having any chance of being saved. Each man determines his own destiny by his reaction to God's offer of mercy, whether it be in the redeeming Gospel of Christ, or in His revelation of Himself in nature, which all men have, and through which God speaks and works.

Man is a sinner, but he is not just a lump of corruption without emotions, affections, volition, powers of determination. He is not a puppet on a string. He is responsible to God, and therefore free in some sense; free to make a choice. Otherwise judgement at last would be unjust. Notwithstanding all the mysteries in connection with the doctrine of predestination one is certain of this: If one man is saved and another is lost it is not because God has acted in a capricious way; it is not because He was willing to do something for the one that He was unwilling to do for the other; it is because the one accepted God's provision in Christ and the other rejected it.

Without doubt the Bible teaches the sovereignty of God. He is the King who never abdicates. But the Bible also teaches the responsibility of man, and so his freedom of choice. Great portions of the Bible are meaningless, indeed are only a mockery, without the pre-supposition of Free will. If one system of theology denies human Free will, and if another system denies Divine sovereignty, we may be sure that neither is completely Biblical. Sanday and Headlam say: 'Paul never says or implies that God has created man for the purpose of his damnation. What he does say is that in His government of the world God reserves to Himself

B

perfect freedom of dealing with man on His own conditions and not on man's' (*The International Critical Commentary*, Romans p. 258). God's conditions are a change of mind and faith in the Lord Jesus Christ. Man cannot come to God and say: 'I'll be saved if you allow me so much credit for my good works, or if you treat me differently from others who are more sinful than I'. God dictates the terms. He offers salvation as the unmerited gift of His sovereign grace. It is a Divine gift, and it has to be taken by faith. Savlation cannot be achieved by good works.

After a good deal of reading about Free will and Divine sovereignty one agrees wholeheartedly with Sanday and Headlam when they say: 'The two ideas of Free will and Divine sovereignty cannot be reconciled in our own mind, but that does not prevent them from being reconciled in God's mind. We are really measuring Him by our own intellectual standard if we think otherwise. And so our solution of the problem of Free will, and of the problems of history and of individual salvation, must finally lie in the full acceptance and realization of what is implied by the infinity and the omniscience of God' (*The International Critical Commentary*, Romans p. 350).

In his fine book, *The Christian Religion in its Doctrinal Expression*, Dr E.Y. Mullins says: 'God's providential control of the world respects human freedom. Man is distinguished from physical nature by the possession of free personality . . . God has limited himself in his methods with free beings. Here compulsion is out of the question. Sovereignty and predestination do not annul freedom. If they did so, man would be reduced to the physical, or at least the brute, level. God does not indeed surrender the destinies of the universe to his free creatures. But his control is through means which have respect for their freedom' (p.268). Man is always man, distinct from every other part of creation in that he has personality, self-consciousness and self-determination. What sinful men do on the earth, however mighty, cannot dethrone God. He still reigns when man has done his worst. His throne is above the powers of men to destroy, but we mustn't conclude from this that everything that happens on the earth, all the tragedies, all the sin, all the wars, all the suffering, all the grasping after material things is according to the *directive* will of God, that all are *caused* by God. Since God denounces sin and calls men to repentance, a change of mind, and faith in Christ, it follows that His will is not being done. He permits many things which He doesn't cause, otherwise we make Him the author of evil.

Our Lord was crucified by wicked men. Peter charged the people with killing the Prince of Life. Christ prayed: 'Father, forgive them for they know not what they do' (Luke 23:34). If the crucifiers of the Son of God had been doing the will of God, He would have prayed: 'Father, reward them for they have done Thy will'. The crucifixion of the Son of God remains the supreme crime of the human race. We should be clear in our minds that the cruelties meted out to Christ by wicked men did not constitute the Atonement. We are saved not by what wicked men did to Christ, but by what God in Christ did. Some never get away from the physical sufferings of Christ to the deeper truth of His spiritual sufferings, His suffering at the hand of God. God laying on Christ the iniquities of us all; God in Christ bearing His own penalty on human sin, was the

Atonement. This would have been made even if man had not crucified Christ. God predicts what He allows man to do, but He doesn't inspire men to do the evil things which are predicted.

The Love of God

In John 3:16, we have the very essence of the Gospel. 'For God so loved the world, that He gave His only begotten Son, that whosoever believeth in Him should not perish, but have everlasting life'. This has been well called 'The Gospel in a nut-shell'. In John 3:16, we have the universal sweep of the Divine love. It is the whole world of lost and sinning humanity that God loves. The Divine love takes in everyone and leaves out no one. The glory and wonder of the Gospel message is that there is no one in all the world, however sinful and insignificant, to whom we cannot say: 'Friend, God loves you and Christ died for you'. Any theology which denies the universal sweep of the Divine love is away from the New Testament and therefore is not of God. John 3:16 does not say that God loves some men in every continent in the world, some men of every class and colour and clime. It says that He loves the whole world, all men and women everywhere. We mustn't alter the word of God to suit our theological theories. The love of God is a world-embracing, wondrous love, a love unsought and unbought, a love that doesn't leave out anyone because of race or colour or condition. This is the full content of the Gospel, and it is worthy of the glory and greatness of God. It magnifies His grace and love.

Browning wrote: 'God! Thou art Love! I build my faith on that'. He is love, but he is also holy, just, righteous, and the Judge of all. In John 3:16, we have the supreme expression of the Divine love. God so loved that He gave His only begotten Son. He gave the best gift He could give, His only begotten and well-beloved Son, the one who was in His bosom, the place of affection and fellowship, from all eternity. It was not the highest and greatest of created beings that God gave, but His well-beloved Son, co-equal and co-eternal with Him. The term 'only begotten' means the only one of its kind. We have the absolute uniqueness of Christ. He was uncreated, and He created all things. Think of the One whom God gave, and think of the ones for whom He gave Him and you see the wonder of the Divine love. On John 3:16, Dr A.T. Robertson says: 'The world (Ton kosmon), the whole kosmos of men, including Gentiles, the whole human race. This universal aspect of God's love appears also in 2 Cor. 5:19; Rom. 5:8)'. On John 3:16 Bishop Westcott says: 'Loved *the world*, loved all humanity considered as apart from himself'. Exegesis must determine theology, not theology exegesis. We mustn't come to the Scriptures with dogmatic, theological pre-suppositions. We must come to the Word of God with minds free and ready to accept what the Holy Spirit teaches.

To accept the theology that God loves only those whom He elects to save, and then interpret 'world' in John 3:16 as 'elect' or as 'some', is not allowing the Scriptures to speak for themselves. It is really altering the Scriptures to suit a theological theory. The word of God has a way of upsetting the systems of men. If either our Lord or the Apostle John had meant to teach that God's love is limited to some who are His favourites, and that He excludes all others, they would have said so without ambiguity. We would have read something like this: 'For God so loved *the elect*, that He gave His only begotten Son that those to whom He gives faith might not perish but have everlasting life'. The fact that John 3:16 doesn't say this, is proof that neither our Lord nor His inspired Apostle meant it. They meant to teach the universality of the Divine love.

We thank God that we have a Gospel, good news, for all men everywhere, whatever their colour, class, creed, or condition. This is the distinctive glory of the Christian message, and it makes Christianity unique. If any perish, it is not because God doesn't love them; it is not because Christ didn't die for them; it is not because salvation hasn't been provided for them at infinite cost; it is because they have deliberately and persistently rejected it. The atoning work of Christ is the supreme proof of the Divine love. Dr James Denney says: 'If the propitiatory death of Christ is eliminated from the love of God, it might be unfair to say that the love of God is robbed of all meaning, but it is certainly robbed of its apostolic meaning' (*The Death of Christ* p. 276). 'Hereby perceive we the love of God, because he laid down his life for us' (1 John 3:16). God loves all sinners, not because Christ died for them, but Christ died for them because God loved them. No one lies outside the scope of the Divine love. Dr James Denney says: 'It is not in Christ being here, but in His being here as a propitiation for the sins of the world, that the love of God is revealed. Not Bethlehem, but Calvary is the focus of revelation' (*The Death of Christ* p. 324 and 325). Of the liberal theologians of his day, Dr Denney wrote: 'God is love, they say, and therefore He does *not require* a propitiation. God is love, say the apostles, and therefore He *provides* a propitiation'.

That God is love involves the possibility of Divine suffering. Love and impassibility are mutually exclusive. If God is love He suffers; if He doesn't suffer He isn't love. God in Christ suffering for sinful men is the Atonement. Some think that God is so majestic, so transcendent, so outside time and space that He is incapable of suffering. But the Bible attributes to God the emotion of grief. Genesis 6:6 says: 'It grieved Him at His heart'. 'It pained Him at His heart'. He feels because He loves. Isaiah 63:9 says: 'In all their afflictions he was afflicted'. 'There is no place where earth's sorrows are more felt than up in heaven'. Dr A.H. Strong says: 'Jesus Christ in his sorrow and sympathy, his tears and agony, is the revealer of God's feelings toward the race, and we are urged to follow in his steps, that we may be perfect, as our Father in heaven is perfect. We cannot indeed conceive of love without self-sacrifice, nor of self-sacrifice without suffering' (*Systematic Theology* p. 266). He says that the blessedness of God is consistent with emotions of sorrow. The denial of the possibility of Divine suffering, undermines the whole efficacy of the Atonement. The best man that ever lived could not have suffered sufficiently for the salvation of guilty mankind. Christ was the God-man, and when He suffered God suffered, so His sufferings are of infinite value.

B.P. Bowne on the Atonement says: 'So long as we conceive of God as sitting apart in supreme ease and self-satisfaction, he is not *love* at all, but only a reflection of our selfishness and vulgarity. So long as we conceive of him as bestowing blessing upon us out of his infinite fullness, but at no real cost to himself, he sinks below the moral heroes of our race. There is never a higher thought possible, until we see God taking the world upon his heart, entering into the fellowship of our sorrow, and becoming the supreme burden bearer and leader in self-sacrifice. *Then only* are the possibilities of grace and condescension and love and moral heroism filled up, so that nothing higher remains. And the work of Christ, so far as it was a historical event, must be viewed not merely as a piece of history, but also as a manifestation of that cross which was hidden in the divine love from the foundation of the world, and which is involved in the existence of the human world at all'.

We cannot doubt the truth of the Divine love or the efficacy of God's atonement for sin, when we see that there was suffering in eternity before there was suffering in time. Dr A.H. Strong says that in the substitutionary view of the Atonement there is 'A moving exhibition of God's love — a love that is not satisfied with suffering in and with the sinner . . . . but a love that sinks itself into the sinner's guilt and bears his penalty' (*Systematic Theology* p. 766).

The Grace of God

Paul said that he had received this ministry to 'testify the Gospel of the grace of God' (Acts 20:24). The Apostle bore his testimony concerning the good news of the unmerited, unearned, unbounded favour of God. The grace of God is the love of God in action, doing for man what he could never do for himself and what no one else could do for him, that is, atoning for his sins and bridging the gulf between himself and a holy God. The mercy of God means that we don't receive what we deserve because of our sin, that is, the judgement of God. The grace of God means that we receive what we don't deserve, that is, the salvation of God, pardon, life, health, peace and heaven at last. It is all of grace that salvation has been provided for guilty mankind. Man didn't come asking for mercy and blessing. *God took the first step* and provided salvation for a lost world. It is now offered to all as a free gift. God always takes the first step in man's salvation. He comes to man where he is in his sin and need. He offers him salvation in Christ through faith, but He leaves him free to accept His gift in Christ or to reject it. Dr James Denney wrote: 'Grace is the love of God, spontaneous, beautiful, unearned, at work in Jesus Christ for the salvation of sinful men'.

The Impartiality of God

'Fairness is the touchstone of everything that He does'. This message needs to be proclaimed throughout the world. The God of the Bible, the God and Father of our Lord Jesus Christ, is unlike the gods of men's making. The Apostle Peter said: 'Of a truth I perceive that God is no respecter of persons' (Acts 10:34). On this verse Dr A.T. Robertson, the world-famous authority on New Testament Greek, says: 'The idea is to pay regard to one's looks or circumstances rather than to his intrinsic character. The Jews had come to feel that they were favourite of God and actually sons of the kingdom of heaven because they were descendants of Abraham. John the Baptist rebuked them for this fallacy' (*Word Pictures in the New Testament*). Paul wrote: 'For there is no respect of persons with God' (Rom. 2:9). The Amplified New Testament has this rendering: 'For God shows no partiality (undue favour, or unfairness; with Him one man is not different from another)'. The word rendered 'respect of persons' is peculiar to Biblical and Ecclesiastical Greek and always implies favouritism, to show partiality. There is no favouritism with God.

On Romans 2:9, Dr Charles Hodge writes: 'This verse then contains the sentiment which is at the foundation of the declaration of the preceding verses. The Jews and Gentiles shall be treated on precisely the same principles, because God is perfectly impartial'. Bishop Moule wrote: 'There is no favouritism in God's court. No one is acquitted there for his reputable connections, or for his possession of personal talents'. 'God treats all men alike' (Today's English Version). Since God treats all men alike, He has made provision for all men, and every man gets a fair chance. If God loves one man and doesn't love another; if He gives faith to one man and not to another; if He gives one man a chance to be saved that He doesn't give to another, then obviously He is not treating all men alike. This verse in Romans 2 says, beyond all ambiguity, that He does treat all men alike. In His sovereign acts God never violates His justice or ignores His mercy.

The Holiness of God

Moses said: 'Who is like unto thee, O Lord, among the gods? Who is like thee, glorious in holiness, fearful in praises, doing wonders?' (Exod. 15:11). The unfallen angels say: 'Holy, holy, holy, is the Lord of hosts' (Isa. 6:3). Some careful students of the Old Testament say that holiness is the fundamental thought of Old Testament religion. No doubt there is the unity of God, the majesty of God, and the compassion of God, but as E.G. Robinson says: 'Holiness is the one pre-eminent attribute of God.

Hence everything divine is holy — the temple, the Scriptures, the Spirit'. Wardlaw calls holiness 'the union of all the attributes, as pure white light is the union of all the coloured rays of the spectrum'. Dr A.H. Strong says: 'The fact that the Spirit of God is denominated the *Holy* Spirit should teach us what is God's essential nature, and the requisition that we should be holy as He is holy, should teach us what is the true standard of human duty and object of human ambition' (*Systematic Theology* p. 275). 'So it belongs to the holiness of God', says Strong, 'not to let sin go unchallenged. God not only *shows* anger, but he *is* angry. It is the wrath of God that sin must meet, and which Christ must meet when He is numbered with the transgressors. Death was the cup of which he was to drink (Matt. 20:22; John 18:11), and which he drained to the dregs' (*Systematic Theology* p. 743). Justice and righteousness are taken by the theologians to be the transitive holiness of God. The justice of God is devoid of all passion and caprice. 'There is in God no selfish anger. The penalties he inflicts upon transgression are not vindictive but vindicative' (A.H. Strong, *Systematic Theology* p. 294). God's love is holy love, and His justice is loving justice. All the attributes of God are always in perfect balance. The holiness of God demanded the Atonement. The love of God provided it. Man has to accept it, and then the Holy Spirit applies it, so that the believing soul is saved. We are to perfect holiness in the fear of God (2 Cor. 7:1). We are to follow holiness (Heb. 12:14).

The Wrath of God

The phrase 'the wrath of God' appears many times in the Bible. We should remember that the wrath of

God is as real as His love or His mercy. It is not anything whimsical or capricious. It is not God in a temper damning some and saving others. It is His steadfast and holy hatred of sin which is the violation of His law. It is the blazing forth of His holiness against all opposition to His will. It is His settled, controlled, and holy antagonism to all evil. Of the wrath of God Dr James Denney says: 'It is as real as a bad conscience, as real as the difference between right and wrong, as real as the consciousness of guilt which is but the echo of it, as real as the spiritual impotence and despair, which are the effects of its paralysing touch' (*Studies in Theology* p. 103). In Gospel preaching we must guard against imbalance; we must not present a one-sided view of the nature of God. We may make Him so austere, so transcendent, so just that we dare not think of turning to Him for forgiveness. We may make Him so gentle, so loving, so good that He never deals with sin or judges the sinner who refuses to repent. Dr Liddon said that 'God could not love goodness if He were not angry with evil'.

The wrath of God is real, and we must never water it down to suit the sentimentality of men; but, as one scholar and theologian says: 'We must never represent the wrath of God as the wrath of a God without a heart'. He is ever a loving God, not willing that any should perish. A modern scholar has put it this way: 'Because God is God, because God is characteristically holy, God cannot tolerate sin, and the wrath of God is God's annihilating reaction against sin'. The wrath of God is the temper of God towards sin, not rage, but the wrath of reason and law (Shedd). Karl Barth says: 'The death of Jesus Christ on the Cross is the revelation of God's wrath from heaven'. In the Cross of Christ, God judged sin. He overcame sin and Satan. God never comes to terms with sin. He opposes it and defeats it. Bishop Westcott says that THE WRATH OF GOD is a distinct manifestation of the righteous judgement of God. His judgement is as real as His salvation. Dr A.H. Strong says: 'God has a wrath which is calm, judicial, inevitable — the natural reaction of holiness against unholiness' (*Systematic Theology* p. 724).

William Ashmore says that Dr Clarke lays great emphasis on the character of 'a good God'. 'But He is more than a merely *good* God; He is a just God, and a righteous God, and a Holy God — a God who is "angry with the wicked", even while ready to forgive them, if they are willing to repent in his way, and not in their own. He is the God who brought a flood upon the world of the ungodly; who rained down fire and brimstone from heaven; and who is to come "in flaming fire, taking vengence on them that know not God, and obey not the Gospel of his Son" . . . . . . Paul reasoned about both the "goodness" and "severity" of God'. Dr James Denney says that wrath is Paul's word for God's reaction to sin. 'Both the righteousness of God which constitutes the Gospel, and the wrath of God to which men are exposed apart from the Gospel, are spoken of as revelation' (in Romans 1).

Sanday and Headlam say: 'St Paul asserts both the goodness and severity of God. He does not attempt to reconcile them, nor need we. He lays down very clearly and definitely the *fact* of the Divine judgement, and he brings out prominently three characteristics of it: that it is in accordance with works, or perhaps more correctly on the basis of works, that is of a man's whole life and career; that it will be exercised by a Judge of absolute impartiality — there is no respect of persons;

and that it is in accordance with the opportunities which a man has enjoyed. For the rest we must leave the solution, as he would have done, to that wisdom and knowledge and mercy of God of which he speaks at the close of the eleventh chapter of Romans' (*International Critical Commentary*, Romans p. 348). The Bible says: 'He delighteth in mercy' (Mic. 7:18). 'Shall not the judge of all the earth do right'. In Revelation 20 we read: 'And they were judged every man according to their works' (v.13). At the Great White Throne there will be no miscarriage of justice. The judge will be omniscient, and all the facts will be before Him. That the judgement is 'according to their works', shows that man is free; he is not a machine that has no choice in the way that it goes. If he is not free and responsible he cannot be judged at last. There is the judgement of God in history, and there is a judgement day at the end of history.

The Final Triumph of God

An almighty God must win in the end. This is good news for the believer, but terrible news for the unbeliever. We need to look up to God on the throne of eternal sovereignty and power. We need to look on to the final triumph of God over all the forces of evil. The paradox is: an unlimited and victorious God is *seemingly* defeated now, and a limited and defeated devil is *seemingly* victorious. But the final battle hasn't been fought. God wins the last battle, and so wins the campaign. The call of the Gospel is to line up with Christ, the victorious and all-conquering Lord, and so be on the winning side at last. Faith holds on to the truth that God wins in the end. Christ will reign as King of Kings and Lord of Lords. Consider this, if you are inclined to think that there is nothing exciting in being a Christian. The bankruptcy of atheism is a good reason for believing that there is a God, all-loving, all-wise, all-powerful, and overruling all to His own glory and to the good of those who trust in Him and do His will. Atheism cannot account for the origin of life. Organic matter cannot spring out of inorganic matter. Atheism cannot account for the operation of law in the universe. There must be a Life-giver and a Law-giver. Atheism cannot account for man with all his distinctive characteristics — conscience, mind, will, affections, emotions, judgement. The very fact that man is so clever in arguing against the existence of God, is strong proof that he was created by God in the image of God. He may use his God-given gifts in the wrong way and for his own glory. Man cannot be the product of blind force. After all, where did force come from? Who or what began the evolutionary process? Who or what keeps it going?

Chapter 2

THE TRUTH ABOUT CHRIST

The Lord Jesus Christ, in His unique Person and in His atoning Work, is the heart of Bible revelation. Away from Him we are away from the source of life, of love, of truth, of grace, of power, and of everything that is eternal. The New Testament is so full of Christ and His saving Work that if we take Him away there is nothing much left. The Bible doctrine of the Person and Work of Christ is the strongest argument for the inspiration of the Book. Man, without the illumination of the Holy Spirit, would never have thought of Christ as the God-man who atoned for the sins of the world. True Godhead and true Manhood are essential to explain this Person Who dominates Bible revelation.

Professor A.M. Hunter says: 'Down the centuries men have reacted in three ways to the *Mysterium Christi*. The Socinians have seen in him prophet and hero, the classic instance of created man. The Arians have found in him God's plenipotentiary — the Superman, the half-god but still a creature. The Athanasians have avowed in him Immanuel, God with us, the Supernal man, the Lord from heaven . . . . Could the sinner's reconcilement with a holy God be effected by anyone less than God?' (*Teaching and Preaching the New Testament* p. 177). Those who deny the true Godhead and true Manhood of Christ do away with the whole efficacy of His atoning Work and leave the world without a Redeemer.

Dr A.H. Strong, after many years of wide reading and theological thinking, declared: 'I am distressed by some common theological tendencies of our time, because I believe them to be false to both science and religion. How men who have ever felt themselves to be lost sinners and who have once received pardon from their crucified Lord and Saviour, can thereafter seek to pare down His attributes, deny His deity and atonement, tear from His brow the crown of miracle and sovereignty, relegate Him to the place of a merely moral teacher who influences us only as does Socrates by words spoken across a stretch of ages, passes my comprehension . . . . What think ye of Christ is still the critical question, and none are entitled to the name of Christian who, in the face of the evidence He has furnished us, cannot answer the question aright' (*Systematic Theology* Preface - p. 8).

Today some think they can have low views of the Person and Work of Christ; can look upon Him just as the highest product of humanity; and yet claim to be Christians. They have no right to accept the high ethical teaching of Christ and then deny His proper Deity, His perfect Humanity, His infallibility, His vicarious Atonement, His physical Resurrection, His exclusive Saviourhood, and His Coming Again to reign. In this chapter and in the next one we are going to look very briefly at some of the New Testament teaching concerning our Lord's Person and Work. The Christology of the New Testament is very high.

The Great God

In Titus 2:13 Paul writes about, 'awaiting our blessed hope, the appearing of the glory of our great God and Saviour Jesus Christ' (R.S.V.). There is no doubt about it the Lord Jesus is here designated 'the great God and our Saviour'. In his exposition of this verse Bishop Ellicott says: 'When we candidly weigh all the evidence, it does indeed seem difficult to resist the conviction that our blessed Lord is here said to be our *Megas Theos* (Great God), and that this text is a direct, definite, and even *studied* declaration of the divinity of the eternal Son'. We would say the *Deity* of the eternal Son, for *Deity is divine essence*, what God is, whereas *divinity is divine likeness*. Jesus was not just like God; He was God in nature.

Dr A.T. Robertson says that 'our great God and Saviour' (in Titus 2:13), is the necessary meaning of the one article with THEOU and SOTEROS as in 2 Peter 1:1. There we read, 'through the righteousness of God and our Saviour Jesus Christ'. Schmiedel admits: 'Grammer demands that one person be meant'. It is God, that is, our Saviour Jesus Christ. In Titus 2:13 it is: 'The great God, that is, our Saviour Jesus Christ'. On this verse Dr Donald Guthrie says: 'There is no reason to suppose that the apostle would not have made such an ascription to Christ if the most reasonable interpretation of Rom. 9:5 is followed (cf. Sanday and Headlam, ICC, ad loc.), or indeed, if the general tenor of his teaching on the person of Christ is borne in mind. The use of the word *appearing* which is never used of God, further supports the ascription of the entire phrase to Christ' (*The Pastoral Epistles* p. 200). In the New Testament Christ is called God. Thomas called Him, 'My Lord and my God' (John

20:28). In the Greek it is *Ho Theos mou*, the God of me. 'Not exclamation', says Dr A.T. Robertson, 'but address, the vocative case though the form of the nominative, a very common thing in the *Koine*. Thomas was wholly convinced and did not hesitate to address the Risen Christ as Lord and God, and Jesus accepts the words and praises Thomas for so doing' (*Word Pictures in the New Testament* vol. 5, p. 316).

Jesus Christ is not *a* god amongst many gods, the greatest and mightiest of them all; He is *God the Son*, equal with God the Father and God the Holy Spirit. It is sound Bible teaching to say that the Father is God, the Son is God, and the Holy Spirit is God, but there are not three Gods, but one God. Trinitarianism is not Tritheism. Christianity is monotheistic to the core. In the one undivided and indivisible essence there are three eternal distinctions. Or better still, in the one life of the Godhead there are three eternal relationships which we call Father, Son and Holy Spirit. God is one but He isn't a monad, that is, a substance or essence or being without any distinctions. One theologian puts it well when he says: 'Scripture sets before us a great mystery, namely, that in the one unique essence of God, there subsist three hypostases, the first of which is called the Father, the second the Son, and the third the Holy Spirit'. By 'hypostases' he means, separate personal qualities. Dr A.H. Strong says: 'We do not say that one God is three Gods, nor that one person is three persons, nor that three Gods are one God, but only that there is one God with three distinctions in His being' (*Systematic Theology*).

In the Great Commission of Matthew 28, baptism is 'in the name of the Father, and of the Son, and of the Holy Spirit'. It should be noted that it is 'in the *name*', not in the *names*, one essence but three distinctions. Commenting on Matthew 28:19, Dr Alexander MacLaren says: 'Does that mean the name of God and of a man, and of an influence all jumbled up together in blasphemous and irrational union? Surely, if Father, Son, and Holy Spirit have one name, the name of divinity, then it is but a step to say that the three persons are one God'.

In Isaiah Christ is called THE MIGHTY GOD. 'His name shall be called Wonderful Counsellor, The Mighty God, The Everlasting Father, The Prince of Peace' (9:6). In the Bible the 'name' stands for the character, for what the person really is. In Isaiah 10:21, God the Father is called THE MIGHTY GOD. 'The remnant shall return, even the remnant of Jacob, unto the mighty God'. Some have tried to get away from the truth of our Lord's Deity as taught in Isaiah 9:6, by saying that THE MIGHTY GOD means Divine hero or mighty hero or God-like hero, or who, like a powerful hero wars and conquers, mighty man of valour. But in 10:21, the words mean MIGHTY GOD. Delitzsch, a great Hebrew scholar, says: 'The name "Mighty God" ascribes to Him in some way Divine Being'. He says that 'Mighty' in Isaiah is always a name of God. 'Therefore, saith the Lord, the Lord of hosts, the Mighty One of Israel' (1:24). The Lord Jesus is mighty to create, to uphold, to redeem, to keep, to restore, to guide, to conquer all His foes and to bring His people safely home at last.

Wolfhart Pannenberg says: 'From the very beginning Christian theology was forced to say both that Jesus is truly God, and, at the same time, truly man. *Vere deus, vere homo* is what the Formula of Chalcedon says'. He declares: '*Vere deus, vere homo* is an indispensable statement of Christian theology' (*Jesus — God and Man* p. 285). When we say this, we are saying what the New Testament explicitly teaches. The bright boys of modern theology may deny this, and certainly they can raise problems which we cannot solve, but of this we may be absolutely sure, they cannot put in its place anything that comes up to the high standard of New Testament Christology, or that gives us an adequate Saviour for a lost world. To deny that Jesus was as truly God as though He had not been man, and as truly man as though He had not been God, is not a sign of great intellectual development. To affirm it is not a mark of obscurantism or of bondage to human Creeds. It is loyalty to the Divine authority and finality of the New Testament.

According to the Chalcedonian Christology, the two natures of Christ, Deity and Humanity, were unmixed, unchanged, indivisible, and inseparable in the One Christ. There were not two Christs, the Divine Christ and the human Christ, but the one Divine-human Christ. At one time the Divine nature may have been more evident than the human, and at another time the human nature may have been more evident than the Divine, but at all times it was the one Divine-human Person — Mystery Sublime.

The Image of God

In Colossians chapter one, Paul says that in Christ 'we have redemption through his blood, even the forgiveness of sins' (v.14). In verse 15 he says: 'Who is the image of the invisible God'. The Amplified New Testament has: 'Now He is the exact likeness of the unseen God — the visible representation of the invisible'. Dr A.T. Robertson says: 'Jesus is the very stamp of God the Father as He was before the Incarnation (John 17:5) and is now' (Heb. 1:3). The word translated 'image' (*Eikon*) involves the ideas of representation and manifestation. In 2 Corinthians 4:4, Paul says that Christ is the image of God, that is, according to W.E. Vine, 'essentially and absolutely the perfect expression and representation of the Archetype God the Father'. Dr J.H. Bernard says that Christ 'the image of God' is the statement of Paul which approaches most nearly in form to the Logos doctrine of John. John says: 'The *Logos* was God', not just Divine or Godlike, but of the same essence as God. We shall say more about this later.

In Hebrews 1:3, the writer says that God's Son is 'the express image of his person'. 'He is the perfect imprint and very image of (God's) nature' (Amplified New Testament). 'He is the exact likeness of God's own being' (Today's English Version). In Hebrews 1:3, it is *Charakter*, not *Eikon*, which is used. It is from *charasso* to cut into, to engross, then a stamp or impress as on a coin or seal. It is our word character or characteristic. The phrase 'the express image of his person' expresses the fact that the Son of God 'is both personally distinct from, and yet literally equal to, Him of whose essence He is the adequate imprint' (Liddon). The word *Charakter* expresses complete similarity. The Son is not inferior to the Father in essence. Thayer says that *Charakter* means: 'The exact expression (the image) of any person or thing, marked likeness, precise reproduction in every respect'. Dr F.F. Bruce says: 'Just as the image and superscription on a coin exactly correspond to the device on the die, so the Son of God bears the very stamp of his nature' (R.S.V.). The Greek word *Charakter*, occurring only here in the New Testament, expresses this truth even more emphatically than *Eikon*, which is used elsewhere to denote Christ as the 'image' of God (2 Cor. 4:4; Col. 1:5). Just as the glory is really in the effulgence, so the substance (Gk. *hypostasis*) of God is really in Christ, who is its impress, its exact representation and embodiment. 'What God essentially is, is made manifest in Christ. To see Christ is to see what the Father is like' (*The Epistle to the Hebrews* p. 6). The mark left on wax or metal is the 'express image' of the seal or stamp. 'It is', says Dr Marcus Dods, 'a reproduction of each characteristic feature of the original'.

The effulgence, the beaming forth, of the Father's glory, the exact likeness of His essence, upholding all things which He created, bearing everything forward to its final goal, and having made purification for sins, Christ is now enthroned at the right hand of the Majesty on high. He is in the seat of sovereign administration and power. God reigns, and the once crucified but now risen and enthroned Christ reigns with Him. Dr William Barclay says: 'Jesus is the shining of God's glory among men . . . . He is not fragmentary and incomplete; He is the full and exact expression of God . . . . The glory of God is not the glory of shattering power, but the glory of suffering love' (*The Letter to the Hebrews* p. 5). There is the light of the knowledge of the glory of God in the face of Jesus Christ. In Christ we see the fullness of God's glory, grace, love, power, and forgiving mercy.

The Fullness of the Godhead in Christ

In Colossians 2:9 we have one of the most profound theological statements in all the Bible. 'For in Him dwelleth all the fullness of the Godhead bodily'. The Amplified New Testament has: 'For in Him the whole fullness of Deity (The Godhead), continues to dwell in bodily form'. The Epistle of the Colossians was written specifically to combat incipient Gnosticism, a philosophy with a world-view which sought to explain everything on the assumption that matter is essentially evil, and that the good God could touch it only by means of a series of aeons or emanations. The Docetic Gnostics held that Jesus did not have a real human body, but only a phantom one. He only seemed to be human. The Cerenthian Gnostics believed in the humanity of Jesus, but claimed that the Christ was an aeon or emanation that came upon Jesus at His baptism and left Him on the cross, so that only the man Jesus suffered and died. This was a denial of the true doctrine of the Person of Christ, and does away with the whole efficacy of the Atonement, that is, God in Christ suffering for lost humanity.

Dr A.T. Robertson says: 'Paul met the issue squarely and powerfully portrays his full-length portrait of Jesus Christ as the Son of God and the Son of man (both deity and humanity) in opposition to both types of Gnostics. So then Colossians seems written expressly for our own day when so many are trying to rob Jesus Christ of his deity'. On chapter 2:9, Robertson says: 'Paul here asserts that "all the *pleroma* of the Godhead", not just certain aspects, dwells in Christ and in bodily form . . . . The fullness of the Godhead was in Christ before the Incarnation (John 1:1, 18; Philem. 2:6), and during the Incarnation (John 1:14, 18; 1 John 1:1-3)' (*Word Pictures in the New Testament* vol. 4, p. 491).

Paul here emphatically asserts that all the fullness of

the Godhead permanently dwells, has its home, in the glorified Christ, and therefore it is vain to seek it wholly or partially outside of Him. Commenting on the word *Theotetos* (Godhead), A.S. Peake in the *Expositor's Greek Testament*, says: 'The word is to be distinguished from *theiotos* as Deity, the being God, from Divinity, the being Divine or Godlike. The passage thus asserts the real Deity of Christ'. This is good exegesis by a scholar who had no theological axe to grind. He was bringing out what is in the text, not importing something into it that is not there. Our Lord was and is God, not just Godlike or Divine. The amazing truth taught in Colossians 2:9 is that there is nothing in God which is not in the glorified Christ in fullest reality. All this is beyond human comprehension, but if we want a Christ that we can put into the framework of our own limited thinking we cannot have the Christ of New Testament revelation. We cannot accept this statement by Paul in Colossians 2:9 as the revelation of God by His Holy Spirit and believe in the 'reduced' Christ of modern thought.

In his great Book, *Paul and the Intellectuals*, Dr A.T. Robertson says: 'The whole plenitude of God dwells in Christ, not part in this aeon, part in that. It is a body blow to all theosophical fancies. We have here a flat-footed affirmation by Paul of the deity of Christ "in bodily form" . . . . The actual deity of Christ is combined with his actual humanity in one person . . . . The issue is still with us, the gravest of all theological issues, the Person of Christ. The new Unitarianism is as deadening as the old' (pages 119, 120).

The Son of God

In the New Testament Christ is called *the* Son of God, not *a* Son of God amongst the many sons of God through faith in Christ. He was the Son of God before the Incarnation, for 'God so loved the world that he gave his only begotten Son' (John 3:16). 'The Father sent the Son to be the Saviour of the world' (1 John 4:14). Paul wrote of 'the Son of God, who loved me, and gave himself for me' (Gal. 2:20). In the days of His flesh Christ claimed to be the Son of God as well as the Son of Man. He said to the blind man to whom he had given sight: 'Dost thou believe on the Son of God?' (John 9:35). The man said: 'Who is he, Lord, that I may believe on him?' (v.36). Jesus said to him: 'Thou hast both seen him, and it is He that talketh with thee' (v.37). Peter said to Christ: 'Thou art the Christ, the Son of the living God' (Matt. 16:16). Our Lord didn't correct him, but said. "Blessed art thou, Simon Bar-jona for flesh and blood hath not revealed it unto thee, but my Father which is in heaven'. Christ called God, 'My Father', so He was His Son.

It has been argued, though erroneously, that since God is Father and Christ is Son, God existed before Christ and Christ is inferior to God. But as a matter of fact, a father, as a father, does not exist before his son. He exists as a person, but not as *a father*. You cannot have a father without a son or daughter. God was Father from all eternity. Christ was Son from all eternity. Someone has said: 'Show to me and explain to me an eternal Father, and I will show to you and explain to you an eternal Son'. God was Father from all eternity. He never became something that He was not. Christ was Son from all eternity. Father-hood and Son-ship are terms of time and space used by the Holy Spirit to convey to our finite minds something of the unique relationship that exists between the first and second persons of the Trinity — a relationship of life, of love, and of mutual understanding.

Those who deny the Deity of Christ do not see that the term 'Son of God' is used in the Semitic sense of sameness of nature, oneness of essence. John 5:18 says that the Jews sought to stone Christ because He said that God was His Father, 'making Himself equal with God'. It should be noted that our Lord didn't correct them. He didn't say: 'You misunderstand me. I didn't claim equality with God. I only claimed that He is my Father'. This is what He would have said if He hadn't been claiming equality with God.

Hebrews 1:5 says: 'Thou art my Son, this day have I begotten thee'. The Amplified New Testament has: 'Today I have begotten you (that is established you in an official Son-ship relation, with Kingly dignity)'. 'This day' is taken by some as the occasion of Christ's exaltation and enthronement, when He was invested with His royal dignity as the Son of God. Dr F.F. Bruce says: 'The eternity of Christ's Divine Son-ship is not brought into question by this view; the suggestion rather is that He Who was the Son of God from everlasting, entered into the full exercise of all the prerogatives implied by His Son-ship when, after His suffering had proved the completeness of His obedience, He was raised to the Father's right hand' (*The Epistle to the Hebrews* p. 13). Some have advocated the doctrine of the eternal generation of the Son. However, Dr Marcus Dods says that 'this day' in Hebrews 1:5, is evidently intended to mark a special occasion or crisis and cannot allude to the eternal generation of the Son. He says that God means: 'I have begotten thee to the Kingly dignity'. He contends: 'It is not the beginning of life, but the entrance of office

44

that is indicated . . . . The words, then, find their fulfilment in Christ's Resurrection and Ascension and sitting down at God's right hand as Messiah. He was thus proclaimed King, begotten to the royal dignity, and in this sense certainly no angel was ever called God's Son' (*Expositor's Greek Testament* vol. 4, p. 254). The important truth is that it was not the beginning of life, but the entrance on office. We must confess that we are in deeps that no human mind can plumb. But we must not deny clear statements of Divine revelation concerning the eternal Godhead of Christ. His true Deity and His sinless humanity put Him in a category of His own. He is more than the wisest and best of all religious leaders. He was God's eternal Son incarnate for man's redemption. Take this truth away and you may as well throw the New Testament overboard, and chart the religious sea alone.

The Lord

In the A.V. the word 'Lord' usually translates the Greek word *Kurios*. In the Septuagint, the Greek Version of the Old Testament, *Kurios* is used to translate the Hebrew *Adonai*, which the Jews substituted in reading for *Yahweh*, the ineffable name, which they deemed too sacred to pronounce. In the New Testament *Kurios* is applied to God the Father. 'Lord, thou art God, which hast made heaven and earth, and the sea, and all that in them is' (Acts 4:24). Mostly in the New Testament *Kurios* is employed to designate Christ. He is 'Our Lord Jesus Christ'. Paul called Him, 'Christ Jesus the Lord' (Col. 2:6), literally, 'the Christ, Jesus, the Lord'. The title *Kurios* was deliberately transferred by the early Christians to

Christ, to show that they worshipped Him as God. It was no super-man that they followed and worshipped, but the reigning God-man.

The acknowledgement of Christ as Lord is the distinguishing mark of the true Christian, the genuine believer. G.W. Stewart, in the *Dictionary of the Apostolic Church*, points out that in the New Testament quotations from the Old Testament which manifestly refer to God are immediately applied to Christ. The Lord Jesus of the New Testament is on a footing of absolute equality with the Jehovah of the Old Testament. Because Christians, in the early days of the Church, said, 'Lord Jesus', instead of 'Lord Caesar', they went out to seal their testimony with blood. In the early days of Christianity it was a costly thing to say, 'LORD JESUS'.

The decree of God is that all shall bow in acknowledgement of the sovereign Lord-ship of Christ. Paul says: 'That at the name of Jesus every knee should bow, of things in heaven, and things in earth, and things under the earth; And that every tongue should confess that Jesus Christ is Lord, to the glory of God the Father' (Philem. 2:10,11). Peter said: 'God hath made that same Jesus, whom ye have crucified, both Lord and Christ' (Acts 2:36). Kennedy laments that the term Lord has become one of the most lifeless in the Christian vocabulary, whereas it really declares the true character and dignity of Jesus Christ, and is 'the basis and the object of worship'. Because of His self-humbling, because of His obedience unto death, because He finished the work that the Father gave Him to do, God has given Christ the name that is above every name. Some think that this is the name which no man knows but He Himself (Rev. 19:12). Since the name stands for the character of the person, what he really is, 'a name which no man knows but Himself' may not be any specific name, but it means that all Christ is far surpasses human comprehension. God has given Christ supreme authority, and to Him every knee shall bow, and every tongue confess Him Lord. This does not mean universal salvation. Those who refuse to acknowledge Jesus Christ as Lord and Saviour now, shall be compelled to bow to His supremacy, without being themselves saved. The devil and fallen angels will bow to the Lord-ship of Christ, but they will not be changed thereby. Before there can be personal salvation in Christ, there must be first of all an acknowledgement of need, and then a free acceptance of Christ as Saviour and Lord. Without this, religion is only mechanical, not spiritual; it is without any true meaning. The sovereign Lord waits for the surrender of the will and the trust of the heart, before He bestows salvation.

The Lord-ship of Christ in the Church and in the Christian life means that His word is final. When He speaks that is the end of all controversy. God says: 'This is my beloved Son, in whom I am well pleased, hear ye him' (Matt. 17:5). When His commands are obeyed blessing is enjoyed. In the Church in the past, there has been too much reference to the opinions and teachings of men, and not enough unquestioning obedience to Christ as Lord. In all things He should have the pre-eminence. He brooks no rival. He will be Lord of all or He will not be Lord at all. He shares the throne of sovereignty with no one.

The Logos (word)
John says: 'In the beginning was the Word, and the

Word was with God, and the Word was God' (1:1). *The Prologue to John's Gospel is the profoundest piece of writing in all literature*. The Apostle lifts the word LOGOS out of the realm of human speculation and sets it in the realm of Divine revelation. Philo, the Jewish-Alexandrian philosopher, developed a speculative doctrine of the Logos, the Divine reason. The scholars tell us that a comparison of John's doctrine of the Logos with that of Philo's presents a marked contrast. Dr E.Y. Mullins says: 'In Philo the idea is abstract, speculative, variable in meaning, and bound up with the intellectual attempts to explain the divine being. In John the idea is very definite, ethical, and inspired by the historic facts as to Jesus, and bound up with the redemptive aim of the Gospel' (*The Christian Religion in its Doctrinal Expression* p. 161). In John's Gospel we have both history and interpretation. We are told that Philo characterized the Logos as inferior to God because the *Logos* is not without beginning. The *Logos* in John is not 'world reason', not 'the natural law holding the cosmos together', not 'the law that reigns supreme over what happens in the world', not 'That which consolidates the world into a unity', not 'the guide to true being', not 'a middle being between the transcendent God and the world', not 'the first of God's creatures'. The *Logos*, according to John, is a real person on an equality with God, active in creation, and became incarnate for man's redemption. 'In the beginning was the Word'. There was the beginning of all things, but before there was any beginning, there was the *Logos*, Who had no beginning, and Who was the beginning of all beginnings before there was any sin. 'All things were made by Him; and without Him was not anything made that was made' (John 1:3). 'For by him were all things created, that are in heaven, and that are in earth, visible and invisible, whether they be thrones, or dominions, or principalities, or powers: all things were created by him and for him' (Col. 1:15). This is the refutation of a lot of human speculation, and it exalts Christ far above all created beings.

'The Word was with God'. This teaches the distinct personality of the Word. In the Greek it is the preposition *Pros*. The scholars say that it means face to face with God. 'The personal being of the Word was realized in active intercourse with, and in perfect communion with God' (Westcott). The New Testament says that Christ came out *from beside* God. In His great high priestly prayer our Lord said: 'For I have given unto them the words which thou gavest me; and they have received them, and have known surely that I came out from Thee' (John 17:8). It is *Para*, which means beside, alongside. Before the Incarnation Christ, the Son of God, was in the bosom of the Father, the place of fondest affection, the place of closest communion, the place of fullest knowledge, the place that no one else ever occupied, and the place that no one else will ever occupy. Before there was any beginning the *Logos*, the Word, WAS. 'The verb *was*', says Dr Westcott, 'does not express a completed past, but rather a continuous state. The imperfect tense of the original suggests in this relation, as far as human language can do so, the notion of absolute, supra-temporal, existence' (*Gospel of St. John* p. 2).

Dr A.H. Strong says that Christ is the *Logos*, the immanent God, and the life of the universe. The universe must be recognized as created, upheld, and governed, by the same Being Who, in the course of history, was manifest in sinless humanity, and Who made Atonement for human sin by His death on Calvary. We live, and move, and have our being in Christ, the *Logos*, by Whom all things were created originally, by Whom all things are held together now, and by Whom all things will be consummated. This is no ordinary person, no limited, erring mortal, no created god. This is the Eternal Son of God Who became incarnate for the salvation of men, Who died as an Atonement for the sins of the whole world, Who conquered death and the devil and Who lives in the power of an indissoluble life. He is able to save with an everlasting salvation.

The Word was God

John says: 'And the Word was God' (1:1). Westcott says: 'The predicate (God) stands emphatically first, as in 4:24. It is necessarily without the article (*Theos*, not *Ho Theos*) inasmuch as it describes the nature of the Word and does not identify His Person. It would be pure Sabellianism to say "the Word was Ho Theos". No idea of inferiority of nature is suggested by the form of expression, which simply affirms the true deity of the Word' (*Gospel of St. John* p. 3). Jehovah's Witnesses make a lot out of the absence of the article in John 1:1 in order to disprove the true Deity of Christ. Their translation of the verse is: 'Originally the Word was, and the Word was with God, and the Word was a god'. This shows that they know little about Greek grammar, and less about New Testament theology. As a matter of fact the noun can be definite without the article. We have that in John 1:5 where we read: 'There was a man sent from God, whose name was John'. There is no article with God. Jehovah's

D

Witnesses wouldn't ask us to believe that this means: 'There was a man sent from a god, whose name was John'. The God who sent John the Baptist wasn't a god amongst many gods. He was the One true and living God of Old Testament revelation. We shall let the scholars answer those who would deny the Deity of Christ on the ground that there is nŏ article before God in John 1:1.

Dr William Barclay, whose knowledge of Greek no one will dispute, says: 'John did not say that the Word was *Ho Theos*; that would have been to say that the Word was identical with God; he says that the Word was *Theos* — without the definite article — which means that the Word was, as we might say, of the same character, and quality, and essence, and being, as God' (*The Gospel of John* vol. 1, p. 17). This teaches without ambiguity the unqualified Deity of Christ. Dr A.T. Robertson says: 'By exact and careful language John denies Sabellianism by not saying *ho theos en ho logos*'. The very verse which Jehovah's Witnesses use to disprove the true Deity of Christ is decidedly against them. It ascribes to the *Logos* all the attributes of the Divine essence. We say that Christ is God, but we do not say that He is the whole Godhead. Sabellianism or Modalism holds that there is only one person in the Godhead, and He is revealed in three modes. Godet says: 'John does not say *ho theos*, for thereby he would have been ascribing to the Logos the totality of Divine existence, which would identify the Logos and God, and contradict the preceding proposition'. This is strong evidence for the verbal inspiration of the Bible *as originally given*.

The Word was a distinct person from the Father, and of the same essence or nature as the Father. We cannot say this of a created god. Our Lord made this stupendous claim: 'I and the Father are one' (John 10:30 R.V.). 'Every word in this pregnant clause', says Bishop Westcott, 'is full of meaning. It is I, not the Son; the Father, not my Father; one essence (*hen*, Vulg. *unum*), not one person (*heis* Gal. 3:28, *unus*) *are*, *am* . . . . It seems clear that the unity here spoken of cannot fall short of unity of essence. The thought springs from the equality of power (my hand, the Father's hand); but infinite power is an essential attribute of God; and it is impossible to suppose that two beings distinct in essence, could be equal in power' (*Gospel of St. John* p. 159). 'One' (*hen*) is neuter, not masculine (*heis*), not one person, but one essence or nature. Dr A.T. Robertson says: 'By the plural sumus (separate persons) Sabellius is refuted, by unum Arius'.

Jesus was Himself God, not just a manifestation of God. We agree with Westcott and Robertson, though Calvin denies that the words in John 10:30 carry this sense. Our Lord meant more than that He and the Father are one in aim and purpose, as an ambassador might say: 'I and my sovereign are one'. There was sameness of essence, divineness, as well as oneness of purpose. Our Lord said: 'I give unto my sheep eternal life'. If He were short of equality with the Father, less than Deity, He couldn't give eternal life to believers in Him; He couldn't see them through all the changing experiences of life; and bring them safely home at last. We need a Divine-human Saviour. We believe that Jesus Christ was the unique God-man, not just God *and* man, not God *in* man, but the God-man. He was true God; He was real man; He was one person. This is the explicit teaching of the New Testament, and it is the faith of the historic Christian Church. Jesus Christ was more than Teacher, Leader, Reformer, Hero, Example and Friend.

Dr A.H. Strong says: 'Distinctly as the Scriptures represent Jesus Christ to have been possessed of a divine nature and a human nature, each unaltered in its essence and undivested of its normal attributes and powers, they with equal distinction represent Jesus Christ as a single personality in whom these two natures are vitally and inseparably united, so that he is properly, not God and man, but the God-man' (*Systematic Theology* p. 682). No one with any knowledge of the Bible and history will say that this is only theological lumber that may be jettisoned at will. That Jesus Christ was God manifest in the flesh and that He died as an Atonement for the sins of the whole world lies at the very heart of things. It is the life-blood of Christianity. *Without* it Christianity is only one of many competing religions, perhaps better in some ways than any of them or all of them put together, but in the same category. *With* it Christianity is unique; it is the final and full revelation of God. Only the God-man could reveal God to man; only the God-man could keep God's law perfectly; only the God-man could bear the dreadful load of human sin and bear it away; only the God-man could meet the highest demands of the holiness of God; only the God-man could meet the evil principalities and powers on their own ground and overcome them; only the God-man can be an effective Mediator between a holy God and sinful man; only the God-man can save all those who trust in Him; only the God-man can subdue all things unto Himself; and only the God-man is worthy to reign over a redeemed universe.

Since the Deity of Christ has been denied it is

necessary for us to look at a few texts of Scripture which have been used against this doctrine. False teaching has been based on faulty interpretations of the Bible. Men have distorted the Scriptures to suit their own dogmatic presuppositions.

Some deny the Deity of Christ on the ground that He said; 'My Father is greater than I' (John 14:28). Alongside these words we must put the words: 'I and the Father are one' (John 10:30). Conscious of His eternal Godhead our Lord could say: 'I and the Father are one'. Conscious of His self-chosen subordination to the Father for the purpose of human redemption He could say: 'My Father is greater than I'. Athanasius wrote: 'The Son hath not said, "My Father is better than I", that no one should conceive Him to be foreign to His nature'. Dr Westcott says: 'It is possible for us to understand that the Father is greater than the Son as Son, in person, but not in essence'. Dr A.T. Robertson says it is 'Not a distinction in nature or essence, but in rank in the Trinity. No Arianism or Unitarianism here'.

Some deny the Deity of Christ on the ground that God is called the Head of Christ. Paul says: 'The head of Christ is God' (1 Cor. 11:3). A special meaning must be given to *Kephals* (Head). The man is the head of the woman in virtue of the marriage union; Christ is the head of the man in virtue of union through faith; God is the head of Christ in consequence of father-hood and Son-ship — eternal father-hood and eternal Son-ship. In the Godhead there is sameness of essence, but there is also rank and office. The Father is the first Person of the Trinity, not the second; the Son is the second Person of the Trinity, not the first. There can be subordination of office without any inferiority of nature. It is subordination among partners. There is order in rank, but equality of essence.

Some deny the Deity of Christ on the ground that He is called 'The beginning of the creation of God' (Rev. 3:14). 'These things saith the Amen, the faithful and true witness, the beginning of the creation of God'. To say the He must have had a beginning, that He is only the first and highest of created beings, is to misunderstand this verse. It is the revival of an ancient heresy. The word rendered 'beginning' means 'the originating cause'. The New English Bible has: 'The prime source of all creation'. Moffatt has: 'The origin of God's creation'. A man can be the beginning of a building, but he isn't part of it. Christ is the Author of creation, but He isn't part of it. He is the Beginner, the Controller, and the Consummator of all things. It is a Christo-centric universe.

Some deny the Deity of Christ on the ground that He is called 'the first-born of every creature' (Col. 1:15). Paul says: 'He is the image of the invisible God, the first-born of all creation' (R.S.V.). Being 'the first-born' doesn't mean that He was born. He always existed. The scholars tell us that in this verse it isn't the partitive genitive, but the comparative ablative that is used. Christ is not part of creation; He is head over creation. There is priority of existence to all creation and headship over all creation.

Some deny the Deity of Christ on the ground that He is yet to be subject to the Father. Paul says in 1 Corinthians 15:28, 'And when all things shall be subdued unto him, then shall the son also himself be subject unto him that put all things under him, that God may be all in all'. T.C. Edwards says: 'Christ is King as vice-regent of God. His Son-ship, therefore, involves that the kingdom will be delivered to the Father. But Christ is also Son, and Sonship implies the possibility of subjection, even when it is necessarily accompanied by equality in nature. His Kingship and His subjection rest on His Sonship. For only the co-equal Son can be the fit vice-regent of God'. The Lordship of Christ is eternal; His rule never comes to an end. Revelation 11:15 says: 'The kingdom of the world has become the kingdom of our Lord and of his Christ, *and he shall reign for ever and ever*' (R.S.V.). There is the throne of God *and of the Lamb*. He was the co-equal Son during the Incarnation when there was self-chosen subordination to the Father, for the purpose of human redemption. He will be the co-equal Son in the eternal Kingdom when all things are put under God, the Father.

Pannenberg says there can exist no competition between the kingdom of the Son and the kingdom of the Father. The Son rules in dedication to the Father and His Lordship. 'The kingdom of the Son is also that of the Father and vice-versa. When 1 Corinthians 15:28 say that at the end, the Son, after everything is subjugated to Him, will subjugate Himself to the Father, that God may be all in all, this does not simply express for us a limitation of the Lordship of Christ by the Lordship of God, but the fulfilment of the intention constituting the essence of the Lordship of the Son himself, just as the earthly Jesus Lived in obedience to His mission totally in dependence upon the Father, and in dedication to Him. Judged on the basis of Jesus' earthly ministry, the meaning of His own Lordship can only be the establishment of the Lordship of the Father in the world, ultimately and decisively in the coming judgement and renewal of creation. As the Son He brings the entire creation into the obedience of Sonship, thereby mediating it into immediacy to the Father. Because the kingdom of Christ thus finds in the kingdom of the Father not its limit, but rather its fulfilment in dedication to the Lordship of the Father, it does not itself come to an end with the giving over of Lordship to the Father, but will have "no end", as the Confession of Constantinople in 381 says' (*Jesus — God and Man* p. 369).

The Lordship of Christ is eternal in the Lordship of God the Father. As second Person of the Trinity Christ was also in a sense subordinate to the First Person of the Trinity, though of the same essence. After He made Atonement for human sin our Lord sat down 'on the right hand of God', that is, the highest seat of authority and power in the heavenly realm. He is next to the Father, but there is no inferiority of nature. One commentator on 1 Corinthians 15:28 says: 'The question here is one of function. Just as the incarnate Son was subject, or subordinate to the Father to effect eternal redemption at His first advent (cf. John 5:19; 8:42; 14:28), and to that extent owned Him as greater, so, coming again the second time for the final accomplishment of that commission, the same relationship continues. The task completed, the Redeemer, man's Mediator, surrenders the kingdom to Him Who sent Him. Their essential equality and unity remain' (Paul W. Marsh in *A New Testament Commentary* p. 410). It is difficult for us finite beings to conceive of it, and it is impossible for us to explain it, but it is true that there is equality of essence with the Father, in that the Son was not created, and at the same time there is subordination of office, in that the Son is *Second* Person, not *First* Person in the Godhead.

The Word Became Flesh

John says: 'The Word became flesh' (v.14). There was a voluntary becoming, but how that becoming was accomplished is beyond human understanding. Dr Bernard says: 'To explain the exact significance of *egeneto* (became) is beyond the powers of any interpreter'. The word 'became' must not be made to mean that the *Logos* ceased to be what He was before becoming flesh. What He was from all eternity He continued to be. Dr Westcott says: 'The mode of our Lord's existence on earth was truly human, and subject to all the conditions of human existence: but he never ceased to be God'. The theory of a contracted or metamorphosed Deity is not according to the Word of God. It denies our Lord's proper Deity and perfect humanity, and does away with the efficacy of the Atonement. Only one in Whom Deity and humanity were united could atone for human sin; only such an one can be an effective Mediator between a holy God and sinful men'. On the clause, 'The Word became flesh', Dr Westcott says: 'The Miraculous Conception, though not stated, is necessarily implied by the Evangelist'. A.T. Robertson says that no intelligent meaning can be given to John's language here, apart from the Virgin Birth. He asks: 'What ordinary father or mother ever speaks of a child "becoming flesh"?' This is the answer to those who say that John says nothing about Christ being conceived of the Holy Spirit. The truth is The Miraculous Conception underlies all his teaching, and it is an integral part of Apostolic theology. Paul teaches that Christ is the Head of a New Creation. If He came into the world in the ordinary way He was only a continuation of the old creation. He was only a sinner like the rest of us, less in degree but the same in kind. His own clear claims to absolute sinlessness implies the Miraculous Conception. Our Lord had no human father. One thing is clear in Matthew chapter 1, and that is, Joseph was NOT the father of Christ. Joseph knew that he wasn't the father of Jesus, so he thought of putting Mary away privately. But God spoke to him and said: 'Fear not to take unto thee Mary thy wife: for that which is conceived in her is of the Holy Ghost' (1:20). Luke was a medical doctor, and he records the angel as saying to Mary: 'The Holy Ghost shall come upon thee, and the power of the Highest shall overshadow thee; therefore also that holy thing which shall be born of thee shall be called the Son of God' (Luke 1:35). 'That holy thing' should be 'The child to be born shall be called holy'. Before He was born Jesus was more than a 'holy thing'; He was a holy Person. It was in the incarnating act, and not later at His baptism or resurrection, that Christ became the God-man.

We cannot believe in the eternal pre-existence of Christ without believing in His Miraculous Conception. He Himself claimed to exist with the Father before the world began. He said to the Father: 'And now, O Father, glorify thou me with thine own self with the glory which I had with thee before the world was' (John 17:5). This was a definite claim to objective existence with the Father before creation. Concede this, and you cannot believe that He came into the world by natural generation. Bible prophecy predicted the Miraculous Conception. Isaiah 7:14 says: 'Therefore the Lord himself shall give you a sign; Behold, a virgin shall conceive, and bear a Son, and shall call his name Immanuel'. Matthew, by inspiration of the Holy Spirit, says that this prophecy was fulfilled in Christ.

He says Mary 'was found of child of the Holy Ghost' (Matt. 1:18). Dr Alexander, an outstanding Hebrew scholar, wrote a learned exposition of the book of Isaiah. He stated and criticizes the various interpretations of Isaiah 7:10-16, and says this: 'There is no ground, grammatical, historical, or logical, for doubt as to the main point, that the Church in all ages has been right in regarding this passage as a signal and explicit prediction of the miraculous conception and nativity of Jesus Christ'. Much of the best scholarship in the world today agrees with him.

Dr J. Gresham Machen studied in a detailed way the subject of the Virgin Birth or the Miraculous Conception and says: 'No doubt one should begin rather with the resurrection, in which the direct testimony is, and must be in the very nature of the case, vastly more abundant. But when a man has once been convinced that Jesus is truly the risen and ascended Lord, and when he has once accepted Him as Saviour, then his faith will be unstable and incomplete unless he goes forward to accept the precious testimony of Matthew and Luke as to our Lord's entrance into the world' (*What is Christianity?* p. 87). Dr James Denney says: 'Jesus came from God, all the Apostles declare, in a sense in which no other came. Does it not follow that, as two of our evangelists declare, He came in a way in which no other came?' (*Studies in Theology* p. 64). Apostolic theology assumes the Miraculous Conception. The New Testament teaches, without ambiguity, the Eternal Pre-existence of Christ, His Absolute Sinlessness, His Vicarious Atonement, His Physical Resurrection, His Mediatorial Exaltation, His Saving Power, and His Coming Again. One cannot believe all these and repudiate the Miraculous

Conception. It is an indispensable part of an organic whole. If men want a Christ without miracle they cannot have the Christ of the New Testament.

'The Word became flesh'. The question is: What is meant by 'flesh'? In the New Testament the word *Sarx* (flesh) is used in a variety of ways. It means 'fallen human nature'. Paul said: 'For I know that in me (that is, in my flesh) dwelleth no good thing' (Rom. 7:18). Edward Irving took the word in this sense in John 1:14. He taught that Christ took human nature as it was in Adam after the Fall, and not as it was in Adam before the Fall. He said: 'That Christ took our fallen nature is most manifest, because there was no other in existence for Him to take'. He said: 'Human nature was corrupt to the core and black as hell, and this is the human nature the Son of God took upon himself and clothed himself with'. The Bible teaches that Christ was 'The seed of the woman', and 'the seed of David'. This was fallen seed. How then can we believe that the human nature of Christ was without sin? Dr A.H. Strong gives us the answer. He says: 'If Christ had been born into the world by natural generation, he too would have had depravity, guilt, penalty. But he was not so born. In the womb of the Virgin, the human nature which he took was purged from its depravity' (*Systematic Theology* p. 744). Believing this which is taught in the Word of God, we repudiate the Roman Dogma of the Immaculate Conception of Mary. Christ was the only sinless one since Adam was created by God in the image of God. The New Testament calls Christ 'the second man' (1 Cor. 15:47), and 'the last Adam' (1 Cor. 15:45). He was the only real man since Adam fell, and there will never be another like Him. Mary, the mother of our Lord, was a pure virgin, chosen by God, to bear the Messiah; but she was not without sin. The miracle of the Incarnation was in our Lord's Conception, not in Mary's.

Dr A.H. Strong says of Irving's theory: 'It contradicts the express and implicit representations of Scripture with regard to Christ's freedom from all taint of hereditary depravity; misrepresents his life as a growing consciousness of the underlying corruption of His human nature, which culminated at Gethsemane and Calvary; and denies the truth of his own statements, where it declares that he must have died on account of his own depravity, even though none were to be saved thereby' (*Systematic Theology* p. 746).

In the light of New Testament teaching as a whole we must take *Sarx* (flesh) in John 1:14 as meaning sinless humanity, the totality of all that is essential to true and full manhood. We must take it as meaning human nature as it came from the hands of God at the beginning, and not human nature as it is in us, marred by sin. The eternal Word, the beloved Son, who was in the bosom of the Father, became flesh. He was the sinless God-man who came to bear human sin in its dreadful totality and bear it away. He did it alone, for He alone could do it. We cannot comprehend all this, but we believe it as a part of Divine revelation, and we proclaim it to the whole world. Here we are at the ever-throbbing heart of Divine revelation.

We can never plumb the deeps of these simple words: 'The Word became flesh'. We can only stand and worship Him, the God-man, of whom they speak. Dr A.T. Robertson says this very profound thing: 'John does not here say that the Logos entered into a man or dwelt in a man or filled a man. He says "the Word became flesh"'. Dr A.H. Strong says: 'God could not have become an angel, or a tree, or a stone. But he could become man, because man was made in his image' (*Systematic Theology* p. 694). The eternal Word could take sinless humanity into union with His proper Deity because sinless humanity was created by Him who created all things.

Before Augustine became a Christian he was a philosopher. He knew all about the different schools of philosophical speculation. In his CONFESSIONS he tells us that there is a great New Testament statement which he never found in any pagan author, and that is: 'The Word became flesh, and dwelt among us'. Dr William Barclay says: 'Since the heathen thinkers believed in the essential evil of matter, and therefore the essential evil of the body, this is one thing they could never say' (*Letters of John* p. 6).

We should understand that the Incarnation was not an end in itself; it was a means to an end; and that end was the Cross, the Atonement for human sin. Our Lord said: 'For even the Son of man came not to be ministered unto, but to minister, and to give his life a ransom for many' (Mark 10:45). We cannot accept these words as authentic and reject the Pauline conception of the death of Christ. As far as the evidence goes Jesus actually spoke these words. Christ was born that He might die, die of His own free choice, die as an Atonement for the Sins of the world. We mustn't neglect the doctrine of the Incarnation, but we must be clear in our minds that without God's Atonement in Christ for human sin, there is no salvation for lost man. The Incarnation of Christ, His sinless life, His high moral teaching, His atoning death, His physical resurrection, His exaltation, His high-priestly intercession, His saving power, and His coming again are an organic whole. We must not neglect any of them or water down any of them to suit theological presuppositions.

The Incarnation means IMMANUEL — God with us. He is with us in our sorrows to comfort us; in our perplexities to guide us; in our discouragements to encourage us; in our weakness to strengthen us; in our temptations to make a way of escape; and in our needs to supply them. This is the practical message of such a profound doctrine.

He Emptied Himself

In Philippians 2 we have the famous *Kenosis* passage in which Paul says that Christ 'made himself of no reputation' (A.V.), 'emptied himself' (R.V.). There is no doubt about it the R.V. is the correct rendering. These tremendous words, 'emptied himself', should be studied in their context. False theories have been based on faulty interpretations of texts of Scripture taken out of their context. We should remember that the context of every text in the Bible is the whole Bible. It is easy formulating a theological theory and then searching for proof texts to support it. This Kenosis passage in Philippians 2 opens with a very strong affirmation of the true Deity of Christ. Paul says He was 'in the form of God' (v.6). Gifford says that *Morphe* (form) is properly the nature or essence. 'It includes the nature and essence of Deity'. Dr A.T. Robertson says: '*Morphe* means the essential attributes as shown in the form. In his pre-incarnate state Christ possessed the attributes of God and so appeared to those in heaven who saw him. Here is a clear statement by Paul of the deity of Christ' (*Word Pictures in the New Testament* vol. 6, p. 444). Paul says He 'thought it not robbery to be equal with God' (v.6). It was His by right. *Harpagmos* (robbery) is taken by some to mean 'a thing to be grasped', or 'to be seized as a prize'. We cannot accept the view that equality with God wasn't His, and He didn't grasp after it. Some take the word to mean 'to hold on to'. We cannot accept the view that equality with God was something that He was willing to give up, or did give up.

Dr F.F. Bruce, a scholar of international repute, has this rendering: 'Though He existed in the form of God, He did not exploit equality with God for His own advantage'. One is in very hearty agreement with this, for it affirms His equality with God; it doesn't say that He gave up equality with God; it does say that He didn't use it for His own glory. Kenneth N. Taylor, in *Living Letters*, has: 'Though He was God, He did not demand and cling to His rights as God'. 'He emptied Himself'. The question is 'Of what did He empty Himself?" Around this simple question the whole Kenotic controversy has fiercely raged. Some say that He gave up all Divine attributes. Dr Thayer says that He laid aside equality with God. Latouche calls this INCARNATION BY DIVINE SUICIDE. Gess held that Christ gave up His eternal holiness and Divine self-consciousness to become man, so that during His earthly life He never thought, spoke, or acted as God, but was at all times destitute of Divine attributes. Gess himself acknowledged that if the passages in the New Testament in which Jesus avers His Divine knowledge and power, and His consciousness of oneness with the Father, refer to His earthly life, his theory is overthrown. We affirm that they *do* refer to His life on earth, and they *do* refute the theory that He gave up all Divine attributes. Being God from all eternity

Christ could never cease to be God, for one of the essential attributes of Deity is immutability. God says: 'For I am the Lord, I change not' (Mal. 3:6). 'Jesus Christ is the same yesterday, and today and for ever' (Heb. 13:8).

Others hold that Christ gave up the possession of relative Divine attributes, that is, Omnipotence, Omniscience, and Omnipresence. But giving up the possession of any Divine attribute would be giving up equality with God. Others hold that He gave up the USE of Divine attributes. He possessed them during His incarnate life, but He never used them. This is coming nearer the truth, but it is not the full truth, for He did use Divine attributes. He forgave sin, and that is the prerogative of Deity.

Others hold that He acted as though He didn't possess Divine attributes. Dr Strong says that this denies our Lord's true humanity and proper Deity, for God is truth and cannot act a lie. When we read that our Lord was weary at the well, He really was weary; He wasn't play-acting.

We agree with Dr A.H. Strong when he says that the self-emptying meant that the eternal Son of God gave up, not the possession of Divine attributes, nor yet entirely the use of them, but rather the independent exercise of them.

The act of self-humbling began in the glory and continued throughout our Lord's incarnate life. When He was weary at the well He was the God-man in possession of the attribute of Divine omnipotence, and so had no need to be weary; but He chose to be weary. Dr W. Graham Scroggie said: 'Christ accepted at the hands of God a dispensation of subordination and limitation'. According to the New Testament there

E

were limitations, but we should always make three things abundantly clear: (i) The limitations were self-imposed, (ii) They never meant that He committed sin, (iii) They never meant that he was in error. He was always the sinless, infallible God-man.

The self-emptying of our Lord has been used as an argument for His fallibility. It is said that He was a child of His age, sharing its limitations of knowledge. As a matter of fact His self-emptying, properly understood, is a strong argument for His infallibility. He was so attuned to the Father's will that He always spoke the words of His Father and always taught the truth of His Father. He said: 'My doctrine is not mine, but His that sent me' (John 7:16). John 3:34 says: 'For He whom God hath sent speaketh the words of God: for God giveth not the spirit by measure unto Him'. Our Lord said: 'The words that I speak unto you I speak not of (from) myself' (John 14:10). In His great high priestly prayer he said to the Father: 'For I have given unto them the words which thou gavest me' (John 17:8). You see there is very strong evidence that just because of the Kenosis, just because of the self-emptying, He was infallible. He was full of grace and truth. He was truth incarnate. He wasn't a landmark; He was the goal. There is no more beyond Him.

The Coming King

The Lord Jesus Christ is not only the God-man Redeemer Who died and rose again, and went back to the Father, where He reigns in the power of an endless life; He is the Coming King. He came the first time to die as an Atonement for Human sin. He is coming the second time to reign as King of kings and Lord of lords. Any argument against a literal, personal Second

Coming would have been equally valid against a literal, personal First Coming. Christianity has had a historical commencement; it will have a historical consummation. Professor E.Y. Mullins contends that the Second Coming of Christ properly understood is the consistent outcome for a religion which began with a historical Incarnation and Resurrection. He says: 'If the religion of Christ is a historical religion, then the consummation may be best expressed in terms of history. The second coming is the inevitable historical sequence of the first coming. The two are indissolubly bound together. The Epistle to the Hebrews has expressed this thought very forcibly (Heb. 9:27,28)' (*The Christian Religion in Its Doctrinal Expression* p. 451).

There has been, unfortunately, a good deal of speculation about the Second Coming, about the order of events preceding and suceeding the return of Christ. But the great central fact of His coming in person is indisputable, if we accept the Divine authority of the New Testament. Christ is coming Himself; He is not sending a deputy. He Himself said; 'And if I go and prepare a place for you, I will come again and receive you unto myself; that where I am there ye may be also' (John 14:3). No event in history has yet fulfilled this promise. The Apostle Paul wrote: 'The Lord himself shall descend from heaven with a shout, with the voice of the archangel and with the trump of God' (1 Thess. 4:16). Dr A.J. Gordon said: 'We must not confound the *Paraclete* and the *Parousia*. It has been argued that, because Christ came in the person of the Spirit, the Redeemer's advent in glory has already taken place. But in the Paraclete Christ comes spiritually and invisibly: in the Parousia He comes bodily and gloriously' (*Ministry of the Spirit* p. 49). The Apostles saw the risen Christ go into heaven. 'As they were looking on, he was lifted up, and a cloud took him out of their sight' (Acts 1:9). As they were gazing into heaven two men stood by them in white robes, and said: 'Men of Galilee, why do you stand looking into heaven? This Jesus, who was taken up from you into heaven, will come in the same way as you saw him go into heaven' (Acts 1:11). This was not a piece of human speculation; or imagination, it was Divine revelation. The same Jesus who went away is to come in the same way as He went. Dr A.T. Robertson says that the fact of our Lord's return and the manner of it are described by the emphatic repetition. He went away personally, visibly, in the air; He will come again in the same way. It is in like *manner* as well as in like *reality*.

Commenting on the words 'So come in like manner', Hackett says: 'The expression is never employed to affirm merely the certainty of one event as compared with another. The assertion that the meaning is simply that, as Christ had departed, so also he would return, is contradicted by every passage in which the phrase occurs'. Leading exegetes agree with Hackett. After Pentecost, when there was a new manifestation of the spiritual presence of Christ; and after the destruction of Jerusalem, when there was a visitation of Divine Judgement on the guilty nation, the Apostle John wrote of the Parousia of Christ, His coming in person, as still in the future. 'And now, little children, abide in Him; that, when He shall appear, we may have confidence, and not be ashamed before Him at His coming' (1 John 2:28). John was writing at the close of the first century, and he puts the Second Coming in the future. It is 'His *Parousia*', not simply 'presence', but His arrival in person that John writes about as in the future. The *time* of the arrival or manifestation is uncertain; but the *fact* of it is beyond doubt. It is clearly taught in the New Testament that Christ is coming in person, that when He comes the dead in Him shall be raised: that believers in Him who are alive on the earth shall be transformed; that both shall be caught up to meet their lord in the air; that His enemies shall be overthrown; and that He shall reign as Lord of all. This is an integral part of the Apostolic Gospel. We cannot accept all men's interpretations of the Bible, but we must accept and preach the great central truths of the Incarnation, Atonement, Resurrection, Ascension, and the Coming Again of Christ.

E.K. Simpson says: 'One transforming epiphany has already taken place in the coming of the Son of God, an avatar of grace incarnate; but, a Second Advent, a more glorious epiphany of adjudication, impends, when Christ shall appear in the glory of the Father, crowned with the full insignia of Deity' (*Pastoral Epistles* p. 109). It is false to assume that today all enlightened scholarship is against this belief. Pannenberg says: 'The ultimate Divine confirmation of Jesus will take place only in the occurrence of His return. Only then will the revelation of God in Jesus become manifest in its ultimate, inevitable glory' (*Jesus — God and Man* p. 108). All that our Lord really was, all that He did, and all that He is in ascended glory will be fully revealed only when He comes again in person. In 2 Thessalonians 1, Paul says: 'The Lord Jesus shall be revealed from heaven with his mighty angels, in flaming fire taking vengence on them that know not God, and that obey not the gospel of our Lord Jesus

Christ'. J.B. Phillips has, 'the terrific denouement of Christ's personal coming from Heaven with the angels of His power'. There is to be the full unveiling of the glory of Christ's Person and the magnificence of what He did when He died and rose again.

Peter says: 'But, beloved, be not ignorant of this one thing, that one day is with the Lord as a thousand years, and a thousand years as one day. The Lord is not slack concerning his promise, as some men count slackness; but is longsuffering to us-ward, not willing that any should perish, but that all should come to repentance' (2 Pet. 3:8,9). If we are inclined to think that Christ is long in coming, we should remember that from the Divine standpoint it is not yet forty-eight hours since Christ rose from the dead, not yet a full week since God created the world. It was a long wait from the promise of God concerning the First Coming until its fulfilment, but at the right time Christ came. He will come the Second time as the conquering King.

Pannenberg says: 'The delay of the end events, which now amounts to almost two thousand years is not a repudiation of the Christian perception of revelation as long as the unity between what happened in Jesus and the eschatological future is maintained' (*Jesus — God and Man* p. 108).

On 2 Peter 3:1-18 the Revised Standard Version Margin has this comment: 'Scoffers ridicule the hope of Christ's second coming. Delay is no proof that he will not come, for God does not measure time as men do. The delay shows God's patience, and his desire that men should repent. Because the day of the Lord will come according to His promise, Christians should await it in holiness and godliness'. To say, as the scoffers do, that 'all things have continued as they were from the beginning of creation' is to shut their eyes to the facts of history. Many things have changed, and changed for the good of mankind. The universe itself, though controlled by God, is changing.

There is to be the consummation of all things. The Bible tells us plainly that the end is: 'The kingdoms of this world are become the kingdom of our Lord, and of His Christ; and He shall reign for ever and ever' (Rev. 11:15). The Bible predicts a glorious future for the child of God, and also for this earth which has been torn by war and the struggle of man for power. John said: 'And I saw a new heaven and a new earth: for the first heaven and the first earth were passed away; and there was no more sea' (Rev. 21:1). Boyd Carpenter says: 'The sea has played an important part in the symbolism of this book: out of the sea rose the wild beast (chapt. 13), the purple-clad Babylon sat enthroned upon many waters (chapt. 17); the restless, tumultuous ocean, now discordant with its clamorous waves, now flooding earth in confederate forces; the troubled sea of evil, which cannot rest, and casts up mire and dirt, is no more to be found on the face of that earth, or near that city whose peace is as a river, and whose righteousness are as the waves of the sea, and whose inhabitants are delivered from the waves of this troublesome world'.

Dr T.F. Torrance writes: 'The sea was the symbol of the masses of the nations in ceaseless unrest, in godless antagonism, and in the deep mystery of iniquity . . . . But now there is no sea, there are no tempests and no storms, no hideous forms of evil, no mysterious depths throwing up their nameless terrors upon the shores of history. It is not only that there is no longer a restless ocean of fallen humanity at the mercy of evil winds and tempests, but no sea at all. No unfathomable depths of the human heart: No unknown quantities: No aggregate of the nations in undifferentiated mass. The new heaven and the new earth are peopled with beings who derive their personal life, individually and immediately, from God, and walk with God in loving fellowship and filial obedience' (*The Apocalypse Today* p. 177).

The glorified God-man coming in power and in great glory, coming to lead His believing people into the fullness of His redeeming work, coming to put down all rule and authority, coming to reign as the world's rightful King, is a message which needs to be proclaimed today with trumpet voice. When Paul speaks about the *Parousia* of Christ he means His arrival in triumph. Archeologists have been digging in the rubbish heaps of Egypt, and they have found the word *Parousia* used in scores of documents in everyday life for the arrival of kings and rulers. The Coming Again of Christ is His arrival in person, and in great glory. It will be the end of the rule of man, and the beginning to the rule of the God-man.

Paul writes of 'the man of sin', 'the son of perdition', the one characterized by sin and doomed to destruction (2 Thess. 2). He says: 'Whom the Lord shall consume with the spirit of his mouth, and shall destroy with the brightness of his coming' (v.8). We are left in no doubt as to the end of 'the man of sin' who opposeth God and His Christ. Dr A.T. Robertson says: 'It will be a grand fiasco, this advent of the man of sin'. It will be a complete and humiliating failure. At first it seems a great success, but it ends in failure, complete and final. The mere appearance of Christ destroys the adversary (Vincent). 'The apparition of Jesus heralds his doom' (Moffatt). 'The radiance of the coming of the Lord Jesus will be his utter destruction' (Phillips). We should be impressed by the ease with which the Lord Jesus overcomes the lawless one, His supreme opponent, energized by Satan himself. He appears, He breathes; He overcomes.

In the light of New Testament teaching we cannot believe that Jesus Christ was just a religious genius, a social reformer, a teacher par excellence; that He was martyred for what He believed; that today He is alive in spirit in the way in which other great men are alive; and that we are to accept his teaching and follow his example. This is not the Christ of the New Testament nor the Christ that the Apostolic Church preached. It is not the Christ that a dying world needs.

Chapter 3

THE TRUTH ABOUT THE ATONEMENT

There is the great fact of the Atonement, apart from any theory of it. The Cross has been called 'the diamond pivot on which the whole system of Christian truth revolves'. Without God's Atonement for the sins of the whole world there is no Gospel for the whole world. Those who cut the Atonement out of their preaching cut the heart out of the New Testament Christianity. Christ came, not only to live and to teach; He came to die for the salvation of men. The Cross was the end in view.

The dignity of the Person of Christ gave value to His work. The question has been asked, 'How could the sufferings of Christ on Calvary over nineteen hundred years ago atone for the sins of myriads of souls?' The answer is: 'Jesus Christ was God manifest in the flesh. The sufferings of Christ were the sufferings of God manifest in the flesh, therefore they are of infinite value'. In all God's immensities there is nothing more immense than His Atonement in Christ. 'The Eternal love of God', says Dr A.H. Strong, 'suffering the necessary reaction of His own holiness against the sin of His creatures and with a view to their salvation — this is the essence of the Atonement' (*Systematic Theology* p. 762).

God in Christ did something transcendent in its nature and cosmic in its range; He did something that had to be done; He did something that can never be undone; He did something that needs no addition; and He did something that has no equivalent. We cannot say that the sufferings of Christ were equal to so much and no more. The unlimited Christ made an unlimited Atonement. The triune God, infinite in love and in power, made an infinite Atonement for all mankind. It is sufficient for the salvation of millions of worlds unknown to us. Not all will accept what God in grace has provided, therefore not all will be saved. There has to be the acceptance of what Christ did, and the application of it by the Holy Spirit. It is not applied until it is accepted by faith.

We should make it clear that the Atonement was made, not by a third party, not by an outsider, but by God in Christ. Dr P.T. Forsythe said: 'The Holy Father's first care is holiness. The first charge of a Redeemer is satisfaction to that holiness. The Holy Father is One Who does and must atone . . . . As Father He offers a sacrifice from His own heart. It is made to Him by no third party, but by Himself in His Son, and it is made to no foreign power but to His own holy nature and law'. (*God the Holy Father* 4). One feels that there is little preaching of this great Gospel truth today.

The Death of Christ was a Sublime Substitution

It was in the room and stead of others. Dr James Denney said: 'Substitution means simply that man is dependent for his acceptance with God upon something which Christ has done for him, and which he could never have done, and never needs to do for himself'. Unless Christ did something for us that we could never have done for ourselves there was no expression of Divine love. Those who deny the truth of substitution need not point to the Cross as a proof of the love of God. Calvary was not a piece of empty play-acting. It was God in Christ doing something that is beyond human comprehension and human computation . Dr Shedd said: 'The offended party (God) (i) Permits a substitution; (ii) Provides a substitute; (iii) Substitutes Himself'. This is the truth which is often overlooked. The idea is often given that a third party came in between an angry God and sinful man and did something that changed God from hating the sinner to loving him. But Christ was no outsider. He was one with God, in His glory, and one with man in his need. Calvary was not God, the angry One, flogging Christ, the innocent One, that guilty ones might go free. God was not just outside Calvary inflicting punishment; He was inside Calvary bearing punishment. The doctrine of the Trinity is such that God could both inflict punishment and bear it.

On the Cross fellowship between the Father and the Son was broken for a brief moment. Christ cried: 'My God, My God why hast thou forsaken me?' But very soon after that He said: 'Father, into Thy hands I commend my spirit'. The unity of the Divine essence was not broken, and could never be broken. One has met this argument and has felt its force: 'You say that God was so just that He couldn't let sin go unpunished. Yet you say that He was so unjust that He punished the innocent in the place of the guilty'. The truth is that God in Christ suffered the righteous reaction of His own holy nature against human sin. Dr R.W. Dale wrote: 'The mysterious unity of the Father and the Son rendered it possible for God at once to endure and to inflict penal suffering' (*The Atonement* pages 391 - 393).

Greg in *Creeds of Christendom* writes of the strangely inconsistent doctrine that God is *so just* that He could not let sin go unpunished, and yet *so unjust* that He could punish it in the person of the innocent. He says: 'It is for orthodox dialectics to explain how the divine justice can be *impugned* by pardoning the guilty, and yet *vindicated* by punishing the innocent'. The truth is that in Christ He Himself bore the penalty. Christ was more than an innocent outsider.

Isaiah 53 is Messianic. Jesus of Nazareth was the Messiah of Old Testament prophecy. Dr F.F. Bruce says: 'The gradual abandonment of the Messianic interpretation of Isaiah 53 by Jewish writers was no doubt due to the Christian application of the prophecy to Jesus' (*The Acts of the Apostles* p. 193). Franz Delitzsch wrote of Isaiah 53: 'It looks as if it had been written beneath the cross of Golgotha and was illuminated by the heavenly brightness of the Sheb Limini (Sit at my right hand)'. Of the application of Isaiah 53 to Jesus of Nazareth, Sir George Adam Smith wrote: 'In every essential of consciousness and of experience He was the counterpart, embodiment, and fulfilment of this Suffering Servant and His service. Jesus Christ answers the questions, which the prophecy raises and leaves unanswered . . . . He comes forward in flesh and blood; He speaks, He explains Himself, He accomplishes, almost to the last detail, the work, the patience, and the death which are here described as Ideal and Representative'.

The obvious absurdity of any other interpretation of Isaiah 53 is a strong argument for the Messianic one, that it refers to Christ Jesus our Lord. In Isaiah 53 it is not the innocent suffering because of the sins of the guilty. That has happened in the past, and is happening today. We may have our problems as to *why* it happens, but there is no denying the fact. In Isaiah 53 it is not the innocent suffering for the good of others. In a sense all Christians are called upon to do this. In Isaiah 53 it is more than the Servant suffering at the hands of sinful men. This is true, for we read: 'He is despised and rejected of men' (v.3). Isaiah 53 teaches beyond all doubt that God punished the Servant. 'Yet we did esteem him stricken, smitten of God, and afflicted' (v.4). Verse 6 says: 'And the Lord hath laid on Him the iniquity of us all'. Those who say that the Suffering Servant of Isaiah 53 is the Godly Remanant have to explain why a righteous God should have punished the Godly for the ungodly. No doubt God in His sovereignty allows the innocent to suffer because of the sins of others, but that is not what the prophet says. He says: 'It pleased the Lord to bruise him' (v.10). There was something that God did, and did for all mankind. The Suffering Servant of Isaiah 53 is the Lord Jesus Christ, the God-man. When God struck Him, He struck Himself. When Christ suffered, God suffered. Fairbairn says: 'One member of the Trinity could not suffer without all suffering . . . . The visible sacrifice was that of the Son; the invisible sacrifice was that of the Father' (*Place of Christ in Modern Theology* pages 483, 484).

In Acts chapter 8 we have the clear statement that the Lord Jesus Christ is the Suffering Servant of Isaiah 53. 'Then Philip opened his mouth, and began at the same Scripture, and preached unto him Jesus'. Dr A.T. Robertson says: 'Philip had no doubt about the

Messianic meaning and he knew that Jesus was the Messiah. There are scholars who do not find Jesus in the Old Testament at all, but Jesus Himself did (Luke 24:27) as Philip does here. Scientific study of the Old Testament (historical research) misses its mark if it fails to find Christ the Centre of all history' (*Word Pictures in the New Testament* vol. 3, p. 111). Dr R.J. Knowling says: 'From the sequel it is evident that Philip not only preached the glad tidings of the fulfilment of the prophecies in Jesus as the ideal divine sufferer, but that he also pointed out to the Eunuch the door of admission into the Church of Jesus' (*Expositor's Greek Testament* vol. 2, p. 225).

Isaiah 53:5 says: 'But He was wounded for our transgressions, He was bruised for our iniquities: the chastisement of our peace was upon Him; and with His stripes we are healed'. The scholars say that the words 'wounded' and 'bruised' mean 'pierced through' and 'crushed'. They are amongst the strongest expressions in the Hebrew language to denote a violent and painful death. Dr E.J. Young, a distinguished Hebrew scholar, says: 'Whether man will have it or no, this verse and the one preceding teach very clearly the doctrine of substitutionary atonement'. Another scholar says: 'Substitutionary suffering is expressed in this Divine oracle in not less than five sentences. It is as though God could not do enough to make this clear'. Dr Alexander says that by 'stricken, smitten, and afflicted' we are not to understand stricken, smitten, and afflicted for his *own* sins, or merely stricken, smitten, afflicted, without any deeper cause or higher purpose than in other cases of severe suffering. He says: 'The hypothesis that this passage has exclusive reference to the Babylonish exile, becomes absolutely ludicrous when it requires us to understand the Prophet as here saying that the people were healed (i.e. restored to their own land) by the stripes of the prophets, or by those of true believers, or that the old and wicked race was healed by the stripes of their more devout successors' (*Commentary on the Prophecies of Isaiah*).

When we come into the New Testament we find that it is full of the doctrine of substitutionary Atonement. In 1 Tim. 2:6 Paul says that Christ Jesus 'gave Himself a ransom for all'. This was taught by Christ Himself, for He said: 'For even the Son of man came not to be ministered unto, but to minister, and to give His life a ransom for many' (Mark 10:45). The ransom was the price paid for the manumission of slaves. The fundamental idea in the figure is that of liberation, so we needn't ask to whom the price was paid. *Anti* in Greek is the preposition for substitution. It means, 'Instead of'. *Huper* in Greek means, 'On behalf of'. In 1 Timothy 2:6 we have both prepositions, *antilutron huper*. Dr A.T. Robertson, a Greek expert, says: 'In the papyri *huper* is the ordinary preposition for the notion of substitution where benefit is involved as in this passage (1 Tim. 2:6). *Anti* has more the idea of exchange and *antilutron huper* combines both ideas'. Nothing could set forth more clearly the truth of substitutionary Atonement. Winer, *New Testament Grammar* (258) says: 'In Greek *anti* is the preposition of price'. Bultmann, *New Testament Grammar* (321) says: 'In the significance of the preposition *anti* (instead of, for), no deviation occurs from ordinary usage'. Dr Thayer says: '*Anti*, of that for which anything is given, received, endured'. Dr Donald Guthrie is a front-rank scholar. He has written a very learned and very helpful exposition of the Pastoral Epistles. On 1 Timothy 2:6 he says: 'The addition of the preposition *anti*, 'instead of', is significant in view of the preposition *huper*, 'on behalf of', used after it. Christ is conceived of as an 'exchange price' on behalf of, and in the place of all, on the ground of which freedom may be granted. Yet not all enjoy that freedom. The ransom, it is true, has infinite value, but the benefits require appropriation. The Apostle is implying here that since the ransom is adequate for all, God must desire the salvation of all'. The richest content of the Gospel is that Jesus Christ, the God-man, made a full and complete Atonement for the sins of all mankind. Anything short of this is not the saving evangel of the New Testament.

We do not agree with all that Dr Karl Barth taught, but for the sake of those who bow to him as a theological authority we give this quotation from *Kirchliche Dogmatik* 11. 1, page 447 F: 'There, where we the unrighteous, ought to stand, there now stands Him, the Righteous One (1 Peter 3:18). And now there happens to him that which should happen to us: the condemnation of sin in the flesh. In His body he bears our sins upon the tree (1 Peter 2:24). He dies for our sins (Romans 6:10). He becomes a curse for us . . . . And all this takes place in order that for us there might be no longer condemnation (Romans 8:1), in order that we who are under the law might be redeemed (Gal. 4:5), that is redeemed from the curse of the law, in order that we might be saved from wrath (Romans 5:9), and delivered from sin, so that by His stripes we might be healed'. Dr Crabtree says: 'Rarely in the whole history of Christian theology has the doctrine of vicarious satisfaction been stated more beautifully or

F

biblically than by Barth'. *We* can say, 'Christ took my place and died for me'.

Christ suffered in the place of others. He was sinless in nature and in practice. In Him was no sin, and He did no sin. As the sinless One He had no need to die. He was not under the penalty of sin, that is, death, not personally under it, but He came under it representatively, of His own free choice. Pannenberg says: 'Only because Jesus was himself without sin can it be said that what He suffered was not the consequences of His own guilt, but that He took His suffering upon Himself for our sake' (*Jesus — God and Man* p. 355). His sufferings were voluntary and vicarious. Christ was not a substitute for penalty, but an equivalent substituted penalty. He bore the penalty of God on human sin. William Ashmore says: 'If Christ was in no sense a substitute, or if He was not co-responsible with the sinner He represents, then God and Christ are participants in a real tragedy, the most awful that ever darkened human history, simply for the sake of its effect on men to move their callous sensibilities a stage-trick for the same effect'.

Dr A.H. Strong says: 'We grant that the idea of substitution needs to be supplemented by the idea of sharing, and so relieved of its external and mechanical implications, but that to abandon the conception itself is to abandon faith in the evangelists and in Jesus himself' (*Systematic Theology* p. 721). James Denney said that substitution means simply that man is dependent for his acceptance with God upon something which Christ has done for him, and which he could never have done and never needs to do for himself.

In favour of the doctrine of the substitutionary view

of the Atonement Dr A.H. Strong says: 'It most fully meets the requirements of Scripture, by holding that the necessity of the atonement is absolute, since it rests upon the demands of immanent holiness, the fundamental attribute of God. It shows most satisfactorily how the demands of holiness are met; namely, by the propitiatory offering of One Who is personally pure, but Who, by union with the human race, has inherited its guilt and penalty. (By "guilt" he means not sin or depravity, but the obligation to pay the penalty.) It furnishes the only proper explanation of the sacrifical language of the New Testament, and of the sacrifical rites of the Old, considered as prophetic of Christ's atoning work. It alone gives proper place to the death of Christ as the central feature of His work — set forth in the ordinances, and of chief power in Christian experience. It gives us the only means of understanding the sufferings of Christ in the garden and on the cross, or of reconciling them with the divine justice. It satisfies the ethical demands of human nature; pacifies the convicted conscience; assures the sinner that he may find instant salvation in Christ; and so makes possible a new life of holiness, while at the same time it furnishes the highest incentives to such a life' (*Systematic Theology* pages 764, 765). We feel that this is profound evangelical teaching that is greatly needed today. Strong contends that there was nothing arbitrary in God's laying on Christ the iniquities of us all. God was in Christ and bore them Himself. As righteous judge He could, and did, Himself bear His own penalty on human sin.

Pannenberg says that Luther emphasized above all the vicarious character of Christ's penal suffering. There is the well-known formula of the 'happy exchange': because Christ bears our sins, we in turn receive a share in His righteousness.

Since God in His sovereign grace and love made the provision for every sinner's need, without anyone requesting it; it follows that He has the indisputable right to say on what terms His provision may be ours — repentance and faith, a change of mind and a change of attitude. The terms are within the reach of all. It is not pay, or pray, or work, but *take*. When the sinner has become conscious of his need, all he has to do is to accept what God in Christ has provided.

The Death of Christ was a Divine Propitiation

This is a big word which is seldom used in Gospel preaching today. When it is used it is sometimes misunderstood. It sets forth the Godward aspect of the Atonement, what Christ did in relation to God. There is objective Atonement. Christ did something sinward, manward, Satanward, worldward, and He did something Godward. God Himself in Christ incarnate, satisfied the highest demands of His own holy nature. Dr A.H. Strong says: 'The same God who is God of holiness, and in virtue of His holiness must punish human sin, is also a God of mercy, and in virtue of His mercy Himself bears the punishment of human sin' (*Systematic Theology* p. 754).

In Gospel preaching this is often overlooked. It wasn't that God was very angry with the sinner, and hated him, and was unwilling to save him, but Christ came and gave Himself as a sacrifice for sin, and so changed God from hating the sinner to loving Him, and made Him willing to save Him. God doesn't love us because Christ died for us. The heart of the Gospel is that Christ died for us because God loved us. 'But

God commendeth His love towards us, in that, while we were yet sinners, Christ died for us' (Rom. 5:8). Christ died for the whole world because God loved the whole world of sinful and sinning humanity. A mother took her little girl to a Gospel meeting. The preacher spoke about the wrath of God and the sacrifice of Christ on the Cross to appease that wrath. After the meeting the little girl said: 'Mummie, I hate God, but I love Jesus'. No doubt there is the wrath of God, but that preacher had got things a bit out of balance, since the little girl got such an impression. The offending party appeasing the wrath of an offended deity is paganism. God in Christ meeting the righteous demands of His own holy nature that the believing sinner might be saved, is New Testament Christianity.

Lyman Beecher said that the word 'propitiate' is used only in the New Testament in the middle voice to show that God propitiates Himself. The New Testament never says that a third party reconciled God to a sinful world, and changed Him from hating sinners to loving them. It does say: 'To wit, that God was in Christ, reconciling the world unto Himself' (2 Cor. 5:19). Some theologians say: 'God is love, therefore He doesn't require Atonement'. The New Testament says: 'God is love, therefore *He made Atonement*'. This is good news. This is the Christian Gospel. Romans 3:25 says: 'Whom God hath set forth to be a propitiation through faith in His blood'. Today's English Version renders the word 'the means by which men's sins are forgiven'. This is simple enough, and it is good news for all mankind. Dr F.F. Bruce renders Romans 3:25 as follows: 'For He has been set before us by God as the One whose sacrifical death has atoned for our guilt, and what He has thus procured for us becomes effectively ours through faith'. In the New Testament both Christ and His atoning blood are the objects of faith. What Christ did for us has to be made ours through faith. W.E. Vine says: '*Hilaskomai* was used among the Greeks with the significance to make the gods propitious, to appease, propitiate, inasmuch as their good will was not conceived as their natural attitude, but something to be earned first. This use of the word is foreign to the Greek Bible, with respect to God, whether in the Sept., or in the N.T. It is never used of any act whereby man brings God into a favourable attitude or gracious disposition. It is God who is propitiated by the vindication of His holy and righteous character, whereby, through the provision He has made in the vicarious and expiatory sacrifice of Christ, He has so dealt with sin that He can show mercy to the believing sinner in the removal of his guilt and the remission of his sins' (*Expository Dictionary of New Testament Words* vol. 3, p. 223).

The Greek word for propitiation is *hilasmos*. Dr Barclay says that the verb from which it comes has three meanings: '(i) When it is used with a man as the subject, it means to *placate*, or to *pacify* someone who has been injured or offended or insulted, and especially to placate a god. It is to bring a sacrifice, or to perform a ritual, whereby a god, offended by sin, is placated and pacified. (ii) But if the subject of the verb is God, then the verb means to forgive, for the meaning is that God Himself provided the means whereby the lost relationship between Him and men is restored. (iii) But it has a third meaning, which is allied with the first meaning. The verb can, and often does, mean, to perform some deed, some ritual, by which the taint of sin is removed' (*The Letters of John* pages 44, and 45). Dr Barclay says that John brings all three senses into one. Through what Christ did the penalty is remitted, the guilt is removed, the defilement is taken away. God remits penalty because He bore it Himself.

The New English Bible has this rendering of 1 John 2:2. 'He is Himself the remedy for the defilement of our sins, not ours only but the sins of all the world'. This is true as far as it goes, but to our mind it doesn't go far enough. It doesn't express the truth of objective Atonement. God in Christ did something self-ward that the believing sinner might be justified, might be declared free from the penalty of the broken law. God in justice couldn't say to the sinner: 'It's all right, we'll forget all about it'. *He had to deal with sin*; He had to satisfy His Own just claims.

The interpretation supported by Luther, Calvin, Ritschl, etc., that *hilasterion* in Romans 3:25 means 'mercy-seat', 'the lid of the ark', is now generally rejected as fanciful and inadequate. Sanday and Headlam criticize this interpretation, and say: 'There is great harshness, not to say confusion, in making Christ at once priest, and victim, and place of sprinkling. The Christian's place of sprinkling is the Cross'. Dr Charles Hodge says that the rendering 'mercy-seat' is unsuitable in Romans 3:25. 'Propitiatary sacrifice', he says, 'is to be preferred as more consonant to the scriptural representations in reference to this subject, and perfectly consistent with usage'. Dr James Denney says that incongruities are introduced if Jesus is conceived as mercy-seat upon which the sacrifical blood is sprinkled. Did He sprinkle His own blood upon Himself? Denney says that many take *hilasterion* as an adjective, 'whom God set forth in propitiatory power. It is in His blood that Christ is endued with propitiatory power; and there is no propitiatory power of blood known to Scripture unless the blood be that of sacrifice'. A.T. Robertson says that Deissmann (*Bible Studies* pages 124-35) has produced examples from inscriptions where *hilasterion* is used as an adjective, and as meaning, 'Votive offering', or 'propitiatory gift'. Deissmann says: 'The crucified Christ is the votive gift of the Divine Love for the salvation of men'. All that God Himself, in His justice and holiness, demanded, He Himself, in His love and grace, provided for the salvation of anyone who will accept His gift.

Through what Christ did, the penalty of sin is remitted, God's righteous demands were met, the guilt is removed, and the defilement is taken away. It was God Himself, not an outsider, who did it, and did it for the whole world.

Paul clearly teaches that the 'Propitiation', 'the Personal Atonement', 'the Atoning Sacrifice', was provided by God, and was the supreme manifestation of His love for a sinful world. John says that Jesus Christ the righteous is 'the propitiation'; the life of Christ as well as His Work. 'It is more than a completed act; the propitiation abides as a living, present energy residing in the personality of Christ Himself' (Frederic Platt, in *Dictionary of the Apostolic Church* vol. 2, p. 283). Christ died, not to *purchase* the love of God, but to *proclaim* it. He died also to meet a righteous demand of the Divine nature that the believing sinner might be saved. But He was no outsider; He was one with God. It was God in Christ who made 'the propitiation'. It was made by Him, and to Him, and for the whole world.

Dr James Denney said: 'Atonement is not something contrived, as it were, behind the Father's back; it is the Father's way of making it possible for the sinful to have fellowship with Him' (*The Death of Christ* p. 213).

The Death of Christ was an Atoning Sacrifice

It was His free and complete self-giving for the salvation of the world. Hebrews 9:26, says He appeared 'to put away sin by the sacrifice of Himself'. Christ, the God-man, put away sin by the sacrifice of Himself, not some sin or the sin of some, but sin in its dreadful totality. No one can fully comprehend all that this means, but it is a clear statement of New Testament revelation, and we accept it. One day, when all limitations are withdrawn, we shall understand it. Hebrews 10:12 says: 'But this man, after He had offered one sacrifice for sins for ever, sat down on the right hand of God'. There are deeps of meaning here that we cannot plumb. We cannot put the mighty ocean of this Divine revelation into the cup of our finite minds.

Notice four things about the sacrifice of the Cross: (i) the Voluntariness of it, (ii) the Universality of it, (iii) the Efficacy of it, (iv) the Finality of it. The sacrifice of Christ on the Cross was *one for all, once for all*. It doesn't need any addition, it is incapable of any repetition. It is of perpetual validity. The cure that is efficacious doesn't need to be repeated. The teaching of the Epistle to the Hebrews is the refutation of Romanism, and also of some Protestantism. True Protestantism, based on the Word of God, says: 'No sacrifice but Calvary, no Priest but Christ, and no Confessional but the throne of grace'. Some have spoken of the wickedness of God in demanding a sacrifice for sin. They don't see the love of God in providing the sacrifice that He righteously demanded. That Christ was both Priest and sacrifice, and that His sacrifice was unique and is eternally efficacious, is the good news of the Gospel.

After Christ had made one sacrifice for sins for ever He sat down on the right hand of God, the highest seat of authority in the other world. The priests of the Old Testament order never sat down in the sanctuary, showing that their priestly functions were never finished. Their sacrifices had always to be repeated. But when Christ offered Himself to God, the one perfect sacrifice for sin, He sat down. His work of Atonement was complete and finished. 'A seated priest', says Dr F.F. Bruce, 'is the guarantee of a finished work and an accepted sacrifice' (*The Epistle to the Hebrews* p. 239). The resurrection of Christ and His exaltation to the Father's right hand, proved beyond doubt that His death was an all-sufficient sacrifice for the sins of the whole world, and that the New Covenant, made by the triune God, had been ratified. Nothing remains for man to do but to accept Christ and the blessings of salvation in Him.

Christ's sacrifice was '*once for all*'. *Ephapax*, an emphatic form of *hapax*, conveys the ideas of perfection, completeness, efficacy, and finality. What Christ did doesn't need to be done again; it is incapable of repetition. To suggest that it needs to be repeated is to impeach its efficacy.

Professor Haldone speaks of the wickedness of God in demanding a sacrifice. He says that it cancels out His love. The professor doesn't see four very simple, but vital things: (i) God didn't demand the sacrifice from the sinner; (ii) He didn't demand it from a third party; (iii) He provided the sacrifice that He demanded; (iv) actually, He sacrificed Himself. He gave His beloved Son, and He suffered in giving Him.

In the light of New Testament teaching, the Mass in the Roman Church is a blasphemy. The Catechism of the Council of Trent has the following statements: 'We confess that the sacrifice of the Mass is one and the same sacrifice with that upon the cross; the victim is one and the same, Christ Jesus, who offered Himself once only, a bloody sacrifice on the altar of the Cross . . . . The holy sacrifice of the Mass, therefore, is not only a commemoration of the sacrifice of the cross, but also a sacrifice of propitiation by which God is appeased and rendered propitious'. This is a clear denial of the efficacy and finality of Christ's sacrifice on Calvary.

Charles Davis, who left the Roman Church, and wrote a book, entitled, *A Question of Conscience*, says: 'The Epistle to the Hebrews teaches that the work of Christ can be understood as the offering of the great High Priest who both fulfilled and transcended all that was foreshadowed by the priestly cult of the Old Law. His work was unique and all-sufficient, excluding repetition and not requiring any supplement to reinforce its efficacy . . . . Christians have no ritual sacrifice in the Jewish or pagan sense; they have no material temple or altar and, it should be added, no priestly class. Ritually the Eucharist is not a sacrifice; it does not require or allow a priestly mediation by a special class of men. That would be a return to a pre-Christian dispensation. Considered ritually, the Eucharist is the symbolic fraternal meal of the Christian community' (pages 139, 140). We dissent from Davis when he says that the Eucharist is the Christian sacrifice in a pre-eminent sense. The Lord's Supper, a very simple service, points back to the once-for-all, and one-for-all, sacrifice of Christ, and points forward to His coming again. In the Communion Service there is no offering of sacrifice; there is a calling to mind of the only Sacrifice that could take away sin, the self-giving of the God-man on the cross. Dr P.T. Forsyth said: 'Christianity is not the sacrifice we make, but the sacrifice we trust'.

Pannenberg, in *Jesus — God and Man*, says: 'The expiation accomplished by Jesus' death is to be understood as ultimate and final, requiring no further supplementation'.

The Death of Christ was God's Judgement on Human Sin

In 2 Corinthians 5:21, we have one of the most mysterious verses in all the Bible. It is so wonderful that it could never have originated in the mind of man; it is the revelation of God. 'For He hath made Him to be sin for us, Who knew no sin; that we might be made the righteousness of God in Him'. It should be noted that the verse does not say that man made Christ sin, or treated Him as a sinner. It says that God made Him sin. Professor A.M. Hunter writes: 'It was a Divine deed wherein, by God's appointing, our condemnation came upon the sinless Christ, that for us there might be condemnation no more'.

Some say that Paul meant that God made Christ a sin-offering. This would mean, which is most unlikely, that the Apostle used the same word in the same verse in two different senses, that is, in the sense of sin, and the sense of sin-offering. When the New Testament refers to the death of Christ as a sin-offering, it says sin-offering, not sin. 'For by one offering He hath perfected for ever them that are sanctified' (Hebrews 10:14). On 2 Corinthians 5:21, Dr Bernard says: '*Hamartia* cannot be translated "sin-offering" for it cannot have two different meanings in the same clause; and further it is contrasted with *dikaiosune* (righteousness), it means sin in the abstract. The penalties of sin were laid on Christ *huper hemon* "on our behalf", and thus as the representative of the world's sin it became possible to predicate of Him the strange expression "He made Him sin"' (*The Expositor's Greek Testament* vol. 3, p. 73). Conneybeare and Howson have this rendering of the words: 'God struck Christ with the doom of sin'. This is the heart of the Atonement, and of the Gospel. We should remember that we are saved, not by what evil men did to Christ, but by what God in Christ did. When God struck Christ, He struck Himself, for there is the unity of the Divine essence. The eternal Judge pronounced the sentence on human sin, and then bore it Himself, that those who accept this truth may be saved.

Dr A.H. Strong said: 'The unmartyr like anguish of Christ in the garden, and on the Cross, cannot be accounted for except upon the hypothesis that His sufferings were propitiatory and penal'. Isaiah 53 says: 'He was stricken, smitten of God, and afflicted'. Dr P.T. Forsyth wrote: 'There is a penalty and curse for sin, and Christ consented to enter that region' (*The Work of Christ* p. 147). Forsyth says that Christ entered the dark shadow of God's penalty upon sin. If God in Christ didn't deal with sin, didn't suffer the penalty of sin, there is no saving Gospel. Dr Vincent

Taylor, in *The Atonement in New Testament Teaching*, says: 'In perfect filial accord with the Father's will, and moved by the greatness of His love for sinners, Christ came under the curse of sin and shared its penalty'.

The Death of Christ was a Finished Work

On the Cross He cried: 'It is finished'. It was the shout of a victor. It is one word in the Greek, and it is in the perfect tense. It was finished, it is finished, and it always will be finished. 'It is perfectly perfect', says one scholar. Professor A.M. Hunter says that Christ meant: 'I have drained the cup. I have travelled the road. I have paid the price' (*Teaching and Preaching the New Testament* pages 101-104). He drained the cup of suffering that the Father gave Him to drink. He travelled the lonely road of rejection and death. He paid the awful price of man's redemption. The Gospel of the New Testament is the good news of Christ's finished work. Nothing needs to be added to it, and nothing should be taken from it. All that is needed is a glad, personal acceptance of it, an absolute resting upon it for salvation. Those who say that works of human merit have to be added to the finished work of Christ, impeach its completeness, all-sufficiency, and finality. In Gospel preaching we say: 'The greatest sin of all is the rejection of the Cross work of Christ as the only means of salvation'. Dr James Denney said: 'Unless we can preach a finished work of Christ in relation to sin, a reconciliation or peace which has been achieved independently of us, at an infinite cost, and to which we are called in a word of ministry of reconciliation, we have no real gospel for sinful man at all' (*The Christian Doctrine of Reconciliation* p. 162).

The value of the finished work of Christ is beyond human computation. C.H. Spurgeon said: 'In Christ's finished work I see an ocean of merit; my plummet finds no bottom, my eye discovers no shore'. The God of the immeasurable immensities made an immeasurable Atonement. It is limited only in its application because of man's rejection of it. We say: "Tis His great work that saves us; It is not try, but trust'.

The Death of Christ was an Unparalleled Victory

It seemed to be defeat, but it turned out to be unsurpassed triumph. It was victory over all the organized hosts of evil; it was victory in the midst of unequalled suffering; it was victory in the darkness of seeming defeat; it was the victory of love over hate, of grace over sin, and of the kingdom of light over the kingdom of darkness. Here is a verse which it would take volumes to expound: 'And having spoiled principalities and powers he made a show of them openly, triumphing over them in it' (His Cross) (Col. 2:15). 'He stripped the principalities and powers of their armour, and held them up to public gaze, when He led them in triumph as His conquered captives, by that same Cross of His' (F.F. Bruce). Dr Alexander MacLaren says: 'The figure is that of the victor stripping his foes of arms and ornaments and dress, then parading them as his captives, and then dragging them at the wheels of his triumphal car'. Any honest expositor knows that in this verse, Colossians 2:15; there are problems which are not easily resolved. But five things are unmistakeably clear: (i) the principalities and powers were evil forces under the command of Satan, (ii) Christ entered into conflict with them on the Cross, (iii) Calvary was victory, (iv) God was in Christ in the conflict, (v) the Victory of the Cross is yet to be fully applied and worked out. The New Testament proclaims, in no uncertain way, the victory of Christ in life, in death, and in rising from the dead. It predicts His final triumph over all the forces of evil. The abiding message of the Book of the Revelation, the Book of the Great Unveiling, is that the Lamb overcomes, and He shall reign for ever and ever.

Triumphantly we say with P.T. Forsyth: 'The evil world cannot win at last, because it failed to win the only time it ever could. It is a vanquished world in which men play their devilries. Christ has overcome it'. The victory of Christ on the cross, and in His rising from the dead, is the guarantee of the final Victory of God and of His people.

There is a note of triumph in the Gospel which has to be sounded forth exultantly and triumphantly. The Epistle to the Hebrews says of Christ 'that through death He might destroy him that had the power of death, that is, the devil; and deliver them who through fear of death were all their liftime subject to bondage' (2:14,15). The verb rendered 'destroy' is a very strong one. It means to render inoperative, to reduce to inactivity, to bring to naught, to put out of gear. The present activity of the devil is only the death throes of a defeated foe. Christ is coming in power and in glory to put into full effect the magnificence of His Calvary triumph. In God's estimation of time it is not yet a week since He created the world, not yet forty-eight hours since Christ rose from the dead. High and clear above everything else the New Testament proclaims the triumph of Christ in His Cross and Resurrection, and in His Coming Again. Think again of these tremendous words: 'But is now made manifest by the appearing of our Saviour Jesus Christ, who hath abolished death, and hath brought life and immortality to light through the Gospel' (2 Tim. 1:10). The abiding message of the Gospel is that sin has been atoned for, Satan has been conquered, and death has been abolished. The word rendered 'abolished' means, 'to render nugatory, to frustrate, to quash, to dismantle'. It may be rendered disempowering or nullifying. Death to the believer in Christ is not death; it is the gateway to life that is life indeed, life without the limitations and infirmities of space and of time. It is a triumphant home-going, 'absent from the body, at home with the Lord'. It is promotion to higher service. The one united to Christ has to die, it is true; but he has not to die alone; he has not to die the death of eternal damnation. He dies in fellowship with the living Christ; he dies in the glad certainty of eternal glory; when he dies he passes through the portals of death into the cloudless realms of eternal day where there is no death. His death may seem to be defeat, but it is glorious victory.

The Gospel of the New Testament proclaims Christ as the conqueror of sin and Lord of death. He overcame, and in Him we are super-conquerors. We preach the death of Christ, but we don't preach a dead Christ. He is alive for evermore, alive in the power of an indissoluble life, alive as the Saviour of the world. From the eternal glory He says; 'I am the first and the last: I am He that liveth, and was dead; and, behold, I am alive for evermore, Amen; and have the keys of hell and of death' (Rev. 1:17,18). Christ overcame; and He will overcome. He is destined to reign.

It is contended by some that God, in creating man capable of sinning, created the possibility of sin, and,

G

therefore, is responsible for sin. Two answers may be offered: (i) if God had created man incapable of rebelling against His will He wouldn't have created a real human being with self-determination; He would have made a robot. (ii) God in Christ has assumed responsibility for human sin. He atoned for it in the Cross work of Christ. Every man is responsible for what he does with the provision that God has made for him. Those who are lost have no one to blame but themselves. They refused God's salvation in Christ.

The Death of Christ was for All Mankind

As to the extent of the Atonement there are two opposing views. Some believe in a 'limited Atonement', others in an 'unlimited Atonement'. We object to the term 'limited Atonement' on the ground that it is unscriptural, and also that it is inconsistent with the true doctrine of the Person of Christ. We believe that the unlimited Christ made an unlimited Atonement. Very briefly we want to give our reasons for so believing.

All Men Everywhere have been Created by God

The clear teaching of the Bible is that man is not the result of an agelong evolutionary process which began we know not how; but he is the creation of God. The Bible is perfectly scientific when it says: 'So God created man in his own image, in the image of God created He him; male and female created He them' (Gen. 1:27). It is more scientific to postulate the existence of a transcendent and omnipotent God than it is to postulate the 'protoplasm' or 'gases' which came from we know not where. All men are the creatures of God. They are dependent upon Him for the very breath that they breathe. All were created by Him for some purpose. Paul says of Christ: 'All things were made by him, and for him' (Col. 1:16). So then all men were created by Christ and for Christ. Though man may abuse his freedom in rejecting Christ, and be lost, it is not God's directive will that any should perish. He is not willing that any should perish (2 Peter 3:9). He willeth that all men should be saved (1 Tim. 2:4 R.V.).

All Men Everywhere are Loved by God

John 3:16 leaves us in no doubt as to the universality of the Divine love. No one is outside the sweep of God's love. Some say that the term 'world' in John 3:16 means, 'fallen mankind in its international aspect: men from every tribe and nation, not only Jews but also Gentiles'. This is exactly what the verse does *not* say. It says, 'the world', *the whole human race*. Dr Thayer says that *Kosmos* (world) means the human race, the whole mass of men alienated from God. That God loves all men irrespective of their class or colour is the unchanging message of the Apostolic Gospel. Since God loved all men with an unmerited love, He was moved to do something for them in their sin. He did something for all men that they couldn't do for themselves. Those who deny this have no Gospel for every man in all the world.

In the Incarnation the Eternal Son of God Identified Himself with the Human Race

Christ was more than a Jew; He was the Son of man, identified, not with one race or nation, not with a part of the human race, but with all mankind. Dr Westcott says this profound thing: 'Our Lord's humanity was universal and not individual, as including all that belongs to the essence of man, without regard to sex, or race, or time. The word became flesh, not "a man"'. Dr A.H. Strong says: 'Christ's union with the race in the incarnation is only the outward and visible expression of a prior union with the race, which began when he created the race'. The Bible teaches that Christ is the Creator, Sustainer, Lover, Saviour, and Judge of all men. We have a Christ who is big enough to be all these. Writing of the Incarnation, Athanasius describes how the Logos took to Himself a body capable of death, 'That it, having partaken of the Logos which is over all, might be fitted to die instead of all (anti panton)'. Dr C.F. D'Arcy says: 'Christ as universal includes all men'. He says that the death of Christ has in fact — it is a fact that has stood the test of ages — a universal *efficacy*. When the Incarnate Son of God died on the cross He didn't separate Himself from part of the human race with which He voluntarily identified Himself. He died for all. Dr P.T. Forsyth said: 'The Holy Father dealt with a world's sin on (not in) a world-soul'. This is beyond human comprehension, but it is the full-orbed Gospel of New Testament revelation. This is something that is in keeping with the greatness of God's love and grace; this is something that is greater than all the philosophies of men put together; this is something that should kindle the fires of a holy love in our cold hearts; this is something that shall be the theme of the Redeemed for ever and ever.

Dr A.H. Strong says that although Christ's human nature was purified from depravity, His obligation to suffer for humanity remained. He could justly suffer in the place of the sinner because of His union with humanity in the Incarnation.

'Because of His central and all-inclusive humanity',
says A.H. Strong, 'He must bear in His own person all
the burdens of humanity, and must be "the Lamb of
God that taketh"; and so "taketh away the sin of the
world"' (*Systematic Theology* p. 757).

There are Clear Statements in the Bible which Mean, Beyond all Cavil, that Christ Died for All Men

We should accept them as true, and not try to
explain them in such a way as to suit our theological
presuppositions. Isaiah 53:6, says: 'All we like sheep
have gone astray; we have turned everyone to his own
way; and the Lord hath laid on Him the iniquity of us
all'. We have seen that the Suffering Servant of Isaiah
53 is Christ. Dr Joseph Addison Alexander says: '*All we*
does not mean all the Jews, or all the heathen, but all
men without exception'. 'All we' and 'of us all' are
equivalent. Since 'all we' means 'all men without
exception' then 'of us all' means all men. No one will
say that there are some who haven't gone astray, so no
one can say that there are some for whom Christ didn't
die. On this verse Dr E.J. Young says: 'There is a
certain intimacy in this verse which is lost in the
translation. In the Hebrew it begins with the words "all
of us" and it closes with the same words. *All of us* had
sinned, but the Lord had intervened and caused to
strike upon the Servant the iniquity of *all of us*. This is
not a false universalism. The passage does not teach
that all men will be saved; its purpose rather is again to
draw a contrast between the all, and the One' (*Isaiah
53* p. 58).

Our Lord said that His blood was shed 'for *many* for
the remission of sins' (Matt. 26:28). It has been argued
that 'many' means only some, not all. But some

scholars say that 'many' represents a Hebrew idiom meaning, 'All who will be very many'. It is contended that 'all' may be expressed by 'many' when the largeness of the 'all' is being stressed. 'All' in Ireland are few compared with 'all' in England. 'All' in England are few compared with 'all' in the world. In Romans 5:15, 19 'many' is equivalent to 'all'. If anyone is going to argue from the word 'many' in Matthew 26:28 that Christ didn't shed His blood for all, then others can argue from the word 'many' in Romans 5:15,19, that only some fell in Adam. Paul says: 'Through the offence of one *many* are dead'. He means all, which are many, are dead. 'By one man's disobedience *many* were made sinners'. He means all, which are many, are sinners. We shall see that Calvin takes 'many' in Matthew 26:28, 'a ransom for many', as meaning, 'the whole human race'. Alongside Matthew 26:28, 'A ransom for *many*', we must put 1 Timothy 2:6, 'a ransom for all'. Just as we put Romans 3:23, 'all have sinned', alongside Romans 5:19, 'many were made sinners'. It is the whole revelation of God in the Bible, not isolated texts, which is our sole authority.

Hebrews 2:9 says: 'That He by the grace of God should taste death for every man'. Westcott says: 'Christ tasted death not only for all but for each'. Universality is clearly stated. All that the tasting of death meant to the sinless Son of God, is beyond our understanding. It meant the separation of the Father's face, and the bearing of the penalty of God on human sin. He 'was stricken, smitten of God, and afflicted'. Dr F.F. Bruce says: 'Because the Son of Man suffered, because His suffering has been crowned by His exaltation, therefore His death avails for all . . . . It is because Christ has been exalted as supreme over all that His death is now seen to be effective *huper pantos* (for all). So far as the form goes, *pantos* might be masculine (everyone) or neuter (everything); but since our author's concern is with Christ's work for humanity, and not with the cosmic implications of His work, it is more probably to be taken as masculine' (*The Epistle to the Hebrews* p. 39). Because Christ tasted death for every man, anyone who chooses, can stand at His Cross and say: 'He loved me and gave Himself for me' (Gal. 2:20). In their foolishness and sin men and women may refuse to take, as a free gift, what God in His sovereign grace and love has provided for them.

John the Baptist said: 'Behold the Lamb of God, which taketh away the sin of the world' (John 1:29). The sacrificial nature and atoning efficacy of Christ's death was revealed to John, before Calvary was a fact of history. On this verse John Calvin says: 'And when he says *the sin of the world*, he extends this kindness indiscriminately to the whole human race, that the Jews might not think the Redeemer has been sent to them alone . . . . Now it is for us to embrace the blessing offered to all, that each may make up his mind that there is nothing to hinder him from finding reconciliation in Christ, if only, led by faith, he come to him'. Notice the words, 'the whole human race', 'the blessing offered to all', 'nothing to hinder him from finding reconciliation in Christ'. By faith we must come. Christ wasn't the Lamb for the household only, or the Lamb for the nation only, but the Lamb for *the whole world*.

Godet's comment on John 1:29 is: 'The burden to be removed is designated in a way which is imposing, and sublime: *The sin of the world*. This substantive in the singular, THE SIN, represents the apostacy of humanity in its profound unity — that is, if we may so speak, sin in *the mass*, including all the sins of all the sinners on the earth . . . . It follows from the words: *Of the world* that the Baptist extends the influence of the Messianic work to the whole of humanity'. Westcott says that the singular, *sin*, is important, so far as it declares the victory of Christ over *sin* regarded in its unity, as the common corruption of humanity. He says: 'The synoptists have preserved a trace of this extension of the work of the Messiah to mankind, in the teaching of the Baptist (Matt. 3:9). His call to confession and repentence included the idea of the universality of his message. He addressed man as "men". In some way beyond human understanding Christ, the Lamb of God, the One chosen for sacrifice, lifted the terrible load of human sin, bore it in His own body on the tree, and bore it away. The full meaning of this tremendous work is yet to be revealed.

'Once in the consummation of the ages hath He appeared to put away sin by the sacrifice of himself' (Hebrews 9:26). It was sin, not some sin, or the sin of some, but sin in its dreadful totality. This is what the writer of the Hebrew Epistle says explicitly. Though we cannot fully understand it, and though we cannot square it with human logic, we accept it as the inspired statement of the Word of God, and we wait for the full explanation of it, when all limitations are withdrawn. Here we are in a realm which is above that of human reasoning.

On Hebrews 9:26, 'to put away sin by the sacrifice of Himself', Dr Marcus Dods says it is sin 'in its general and most comprehensive sense, all sin'. Westcott says: 'If the one offering of Christ is (as has been shown by its nature) sufficient to atone for the sins of the whole world, then it is evident that its efficacy reaches through all time past and future . . . . It is assumed that it is God's will that complete atonement should be made for sin . . . . Sin is vanquished, shown in its weakness, "set at naught"'. In Hebrews 9:26, we have a clear statement of Divine revelation that God's Atonement in Christ was for sin in its totality. Human logic is ruled out. If it is brought in, many fundamental truths of the Historic Evangelical faith will have to be abandoned. Karl Barth says: 'Faith takes reason by the throat and strangles the beast'.

In 1 John chapter 2, the Apostle tells us that 'we have an Advocate with the Father, Jesus Christ the righteous'. He continues: 'And He is the propitiation for our sins: and not for ours only, but also for the sins of the world' (v.2). Why did John add the words, 'and not for ours only, but also for the sins of the whole world'? It was surely to refute the view that the 'propitiation', was only for some, and not for all. There isn't any phrase or clause in the Bible that is more universal than 'the whole world'. John says: 'and the whole world lieth in wickedness', or 'in the wicked one' (1 John 5:19). This cannot mean that some men outside Christ do not lie under wickedness, or in the wicked one. Paul writes, in Romans 3:19, 'and all the world may become guilty before God', 'and bring the whole world under God's judgement' (T.E.V.). Isn't every man under the judgement of God because of sin? 'Kosmos' in 1 John 2:2 means all the inhabitants of the world, the human race, the whole mass of mankind alienated from God by sin. If John had meant to teach a 'Limited Atonement', that Christ died only for some, he had only to write 'the propitiation for the sins of *the whole elect'*. Then there would have been no question of interpretation. If he had written that, I wouldn't be advocating the doctrine that Christ died for all. Mark you, John says that what Christ was to him, and his fellow believers in Christ, He is to the whole world — the propitiation, the Personal Atonement, all that God requires and all that man needs.

On 1 John 2:2, John Calvin says: 'Therefore under the word "all" he does not include the reprobate, but refers to all who would believe and those who were scattered through various regions of the earth'. He says that he puts in the words 'the sins of the whole world ', for amplification, that believers might be convinced that the expiation made by Christ, extends to all who by faith embrace the Gospel'. It should be noted that this is *NOT* what John says. This is seeing in 1 John 2:2 what is NOT there, and refusing to see what IS there. It is eisegesis, not exegesis. It is forming a theological theory and then trying to make Holy Scripture support it. John does not say, 'Some people in the whole world'; he says: 'the whole world'. If John had meant what John Calvin says he meant, he would have written, 'but also for the sins of all who would believe' or 'for the sins of all who would embrace the Gospel', or 'for the sins of the whole elect'. Why did he not write this, so that there would have been no ambiguity? It must have been because he didn't mean this. John wrote, 'but also for the sins of the whole world'. John Calvin admits the truth of the saying that Christ suffered *sufficiently* for the whole world but *effectively* for the elect. It seems to us that he gives away the position that Christ made atonement only for the elect. If Christ suffered sufficiently for the whole world it cannot be maintained that atonement was made only for some.

He couldn't have suffered for people without making atonement for them. We dare not impeach the efficacy of His sufferings. They had no equivalent. They are sufficient for the salvation of millions of new worlds, if needed.

The Atonement wasn't effective in my experience until I changed my mind and put my trust in Christ as my Saviour. Though Christ died for all men, not all men will be saved, because not all will accept what Christ provided for them when He died and rose again. I bore my sins; I was under the just judgement of God because of my sins, until I turned to Christ and rested on His finished work for salvation. This wasn't a piece of fiction; it was real to me, and also real to God. We cannot bring in logic and say: 'Why should I have borne my sins since Christ bore them on Calvary?' We have to accept the fact of Bible revelation and the fact of personal experience. Paul says of the Ephesian believers, the elect, that they were 'children of wrath, even as others' (Eph. 2:3). They lay under the dreadful judgement of God. Yes, they did, elect though they were. Why should they have lain under it since Christ bore it for them on the Cross?

The Atonement has to be accepted by faith and applied by the Holy Spirit before it is effective in personal experience. None is excluded from the benefits of Christ's finished work by an arbitrary Divine decree. Provision has been made for all, but this provision has to be appropriated. God's gift has to be taken. In *The Expositor's Greek Testament* Dr David Smith says on 1 John 2:2; 'There are *sins*, special and occasional, in the believer; there is *sin* in the world; it is sinful through and through. The Apostle means "for our sins and the mass of sin, the world" . . . . The remedy is commensurate with the malady'. It is evident that to limit the Atonement of Christ is to contradict clear statements of the Word of God. These statements don't need any interpretation by man to suit his theological theories.

If it could be shown that there is in the Bible a term or phrase or clause that means, beyond question, all men and women everywhere in the world, and that this term or phrase or clause is not applied to the Atonement or the death of Christ, then there would be indisputable evidence for belief in a limited Atonement.

On 1 John 2:2, W.E. Vine says: 'What is indicated is that provision is made for the whole world, so that no one is, by Divine predetermination, excluded from the scope of God's mercy; the efficacy of the propitiation, however, is made actual for those who believe' (*Expository Dictionary of New Testament Words* vol. 3, p. 225).

The Gospel is for the Whole World

The risen Lord said: 'Go into all the world, and preach the gospel to every creature' (Mark 16:15). 'Make disciples of all nations' (Matt. 28:19). Nothing could be more universal than 'all the world', 'every creature, all nations'. Now, there is no Gospel, no good news, for every creature in all the world unless provision has been made for all. God doesn't mock people by offering them something that He hasn't provided for them, or that He doesn't intend giving to them if they desire to take it. Salvation is offered to every man in all the world because it has been provided for every man by God in Christ, and in His Atoning Work.

One theologian says: 'Over the Westminister Confession of Faith you have to write, "The Gospel for the elect only". Over the New Testament you can write, "The Gospel for the whole world"'. This magnifies the grace of God, and it leaves every man without excuse. There are those who say: 'I cannot be held responsible for what Adam did in the Garden thousands of years ago. I wasn't consciously there, and I didn't do what he did. A just God cannot charge me with what another person did thousands of years ago'. Our answer is: 'In amazing grace, God in Christ has assumed responsibility for human sin in its totality; judged it in human nature; and purchased salvation for all men. He offers it to all as a free gift. Now, men are responsible for what they do with what God offers to them in Christ'. There is no answer to this argument.

It is true our Lord said: 'The good shepherd giveth his life for the sheep' (John 10:11). But it is also true that He said: 'And the bread that I will give him is my flesh, which I will give for the life of the world' (John 6:51). He said: 'I am the light of the world' (John 8:12). John says: 'That was the true light, which lighteth every man that cometh into the world' (John 1:9). It is clear that Christ has done something for all men, and that He has a dealing with all men. He said that the Holy Spirit would convict THE WORLD of sin, the sin of not believing in Christ.

In Romans chapter 1 Paul paints a terrible picture of the sinfulness of man — a true picture of the pagan world of the Apostle's day. Let us not overlook what he says in verse 21, 'When they knew God they glorified Him not as God'. They weren't so depraved that they didn't know God, and didn't know right from wrong.

Paul says that God gave them up, but *not before they had given Him up*. All men have a revelation of God in nature. 'The invisible things of Him from the creation of the world are clearly seen, being understood by the things that are made, even His eternal power and Godhead; *so that they are without excuse*' (v.20). This teaches clearly that there is a revelation of God in nature; not the full revelation that we have in Christ, but a revelation all the same.

A great many in the world don't realize it, but it is true that all men everywhere are even now reaping the benefits of Christ's atoning work. Were it not for it, judgement would have fallen upon the guilty before now. Because of what Christ did on the Cross, a dispensation of grace has been inaugurated. Men and women everywhere are given a chance to repent, to change their minds, and to put their trust in Christ.

The question has been asked: 'Can a soul for whom Christ died be lost in hell?' We begin to answer this question by saying that anyone can ask awkward questions which cannot be answered satisfactorily. In answer to this question, if we look at 2 Peter 2:1, we see that the inspired Apostle answers in the affirmative. He says: 'But false prophets also arose among the people, just as there will be false teachers among you, who will secretly bring in destructive heresies, even denying the Master who bought them, bringing upon themselves swift destruction' (R.S.V.).

The Apostle says that these false teachers bring in untrue doctrines. He speaks of their licentiousness, their immoral ways, their dissolute practices. 'In their greed for money they will trade on your credulity with sheer fabrications' (N.E.B.). Born again people wouldn't do this. People of these characteristics don't go to heaven. Peter says: 'They bring upon themselves swift destruction'. This is not some calamity in this life, but endless ruin in separation from Christ in the life to come. The point which shouldn't be missed is that Peter says *Christ bought them*. 'Even denying the Master who bought them'. Peter uses the verb *agorazo*. A.T. Robertson says it is the same idea as *lutroo* in 1 Peter 1:18, where we read that we are redeemed with the precious blood of Christ. In 1 Corinthians 6:20, Paul says: 'Ye were bought with a price'. It is the verb *agorazo*. It means to frequent the market-place, the *agora*, to do business there, to buy or sell. It is true that *agorazo* is not *ex-agorazo* 'to redeem, that is, by payment of a price to recover from the power of another, to ransom, buy off' (Thayer). These false teachers to whom Peter refers, were not redeemed experimentally; they hadn't accepted the redemption purchased for them at infinite cost; it hadn't been applied by the Holy Spirit in response to faith in Christ. But Peter says that Christ had bought them, and yet He didn't get them. They were destroyed or rather they destroyed themselves. On 2 Peter 2:1, Dr Plummer says: 'This text is conclusive against Calvinistic doctrines of partial redemption; the Apostle declares that these impious teachers were redeemed by Jesus Christ'. Whatever one makes out of the verb *agorazo* there is no denying the fact that Christ did something for these false teachers, something that they didn't appreciate; they didn't appropriate. They were destroyed; yet Christ *bought them*.

Some Writers on the Extent of the Atonement
Many scholars and theologians agree that Christ

died for all mankind. They leave out the hard, cold logic of man, and go by clear statements of Divine revelation.

In his great work, *Systematic Theology*, Dr A.H. Strong says: 'The Scriptures represent the atonement as having been made for all men, and as sufficient for the salvation of all. Not the *atonement* therefore is limited, but the *application* of the atonement through the work of the Holy Spirit. Upon this principle of a universal atonement, but a special application of it to the elect, we must interpret such passages as Eph. 1:4, 7; 2 Tim. 1:9,10; John 17:9,20,24 — asserting a special efficacy of the atonement in the case of the elect; and also such passages as 2 Peter 2:1; 1 John 2:2; 1 Tim. 2:6; 4:10; Titus 2:11 — asserting that the death of Christ is for all' (p. 771). The atonement is applied only to those who accept it. If it is applied without the free consent of man, then how is it that so many are not saved until late in life? It was surely not the will of God that they should have lived a life of sin, and Christ rejection, before God applied the atonement.

Norval Geldenhuys wrote a very learned and helpful commentary on Luke's Gospel. On *Special Characteristics of the Gospel* — he writes; 'The fundamental quality of Jesus which Luke wishes to show us is, therefore, that He had come as Saviour, as Redeemer. In the other Gospels, too, attention is drawn to this, but in Luke it occupies the most central position.

'Luke, in addition, lays more stress on the fact that Jesus came to accomplish a *universal* redemption. He depicts Christ not so much as the Messiah of the Old Testament but as the Redeemer of the whole world. Time and again the point is stressed in this Gospel that Jesus offers forgiveness and redemption to all — freely and independently of the privileges of a particular race, generation or merit . . . . So universal and all embracing, according to the Gospel, is the redeeming work of Christ' (p. 43). In a very moving passage on *JESUS IN GETHSEMANE*, Geldenhuys writes; 'In every normal person there exists the urge to continue to live, accompanied by an aversion from suffering and death. Obviously, therefore, Jesus, who was completely Man, and not subject to any blunting of His emotions, or to any form of inward hardening, is infinitely more sensitive in His feeling of repugance to unnatural things. It is impossible for Him, in His perfect humanity, not to experience a feeling of opposition to the idea of impending humiliation, suffering and death. And all this is made the more intense through His knowledge that He is not only going to suffer and die, but that He will have to undergo this as the expiatory sacrifice for the sin of guilty mankind. The holy and just wrath of God against sin, fell on Him in full measure, because He has put Himself unreservedly in the place of guilty mankind. The judgement pronounced on sin is death — spiritual as well as physical. And spiritual death means being utterly forsaken of God. How dreadful, then, must the idea have been to Christ, who had from eternity lived in the most intimate and unbroken communion with His Father, that He would have to endure all this. How terrible the knowledge that He, who was Himself without sin, would on the accursed tree, sentenced like a condemned criminal, be laden with the sin of all mankind, as the willing and sacrificial Lamb of God! . . . . When we hear His words on the cross; "My God, My God, why hast thou forsaken me?" the veil is lifted for a moment once more, that we may see

H

something of what He endured for the sake of a guilty world' (pages 574, 575).

Notice the language that he uses, 'guilty *mankind*', 'the sin of *all* mankind', 'for the sake of a guilty *world*'. Geldenhuys was a scholar, a theologian, and certainly not an Arminian. I confess there is something about this by Geldenhuys which is in keeping with the measureless love and boundless generosity of God.

In *Jesus — God and Man*, Pannenberg writes: 'Because all have sinned, all are subject to death (Rom. 5:12). This is the universal anthropological presupposition under which it is possible to assert that the vicarious significence of Jesus' death extends to all men, since the death of one just man (Rom. 5:6) takes the place of humanity which as a whole has incurred death' (p. 262). On page 269 of the same book Pannenberg writes: 'In His death, Jesus bore the consequences of separation from God, the punishment for sin, not just in place of His people, but in place of all humanity'. J.S. Chandlish says that the bitterest element of our Lord's suffering was that He endured it at the hand of God. 'This Divine appointment', he says, 'and application of suffering is inexplicable except as Christ endured the Divine judgement against the sin of the race'. John Calvin wrote: 'Jesus Christ intervened, and by taking on himself the punishment prepared for every sinner by the just judgement of God, he effaced and abolished by his blood the iniquities which had caused enmity between God and men, and by that payment God was satisfied' (Inst., II, 16,2). In Inst. III, 1,1 we read: 'As long as we are outside of Christ and separated from Him, all that He has done, or suffered, for the salvation of the human race is useless and of no importance'. He says that

Christ must be made ours. He is made ours by the Holy Spirit through personal appropriation. If the New Testament had taught clearly that Christ's Atonement was only for the elect, Calvin wouldn't have used such universalistic language as 'The salvation of *the human race*', 'punishment prepared *for every sinner*'. Richards (*Theology* 302-307) says that Calvin in his Commentaries acceded to the doctrine of universal atonement.

We have already pointed out what Calvin says on John 1:29: 'When he says *the sin of the world* he extends this kindness to *the whole human race*'. On Matthew 26:28, 'For this is my blood of the new covenant, which is shed for many for the remission of sins', Calvin comments: 'Under the word *many* the Saviour designates not a part of the world only, but the whole human race, for he opposes many to one'. On Mark 10:45, 'For even the Son of man came not to be ministered unto, but to minister, and to give His life a ransom for many'. Calvin says: 'The word *many* is not put definitely for a fixed number, but for a large number; for the Saviour contrasts Himself with all others. And, in this sense, it is used in Rom. 5:15, where Paul does not speak of any part of men, but embraces *the whole human race*'. This is in keeping with what we have already said about the word *many*.

Professor A.M. Hunter says of P.T. Forsyth that he was a man of one idea — the atoning Cross. 'But that idea — or rather act — was for him something universal, cosmic, eternal. In the Cross he saw the centre of history, and of the moral universe, and he was always summoning his readers to adjust their compasses by "the inexhaustable Cross"' (*Teaching and Preaching the New Testament* p. 154).

Van Oosterzee, *Dogmatics* 604, says: 'On God's side, all is now taken away which could make a separation — unless any should themselves choose to remain separated from him'. God, in great grace and mercy, has done all that had to be done for the salvation of man. The unchanging message of the Gospel is that a full, complete, all-sufficient, and final Atonement has been made for sin; salvation has been provided for all; but it has to be accepted by faith. William Ashmore says that the Atonement has come to all men and upon all men. The reason why men 'are not saved is because when the atonement comes to them, and upon them, instead of consenting to be included in it, they reject it . . . . They shut out its influences as a man closes his window-blind to shut out the beams of the sun . . . .' Any other view means that the reason why men are not saved, is because God doesn't love them; Christ didn't die for them; salvation hasn't been provided for them; God hasn't dealt with them. This is not the God of the Christian revelation.

One agrees completely with Zinzendorf when he wrote: 'Lord, I believe, were sinners more than sands upon the ocean shore, Thou hast for all a ransom paid, For all a full atonement made'. This is in keeping with the magnanimity of God; it magnifies His love and grace; and it leaves every man without excuse. Stainer wrote:

> Cross of Jesus, Cross of sorrow,
> Where the blood of Christ was shed,
> Perfect God on thee hath suffered,
> Perfect Man on thee hath bled.
>
> There the King of all the ages,
> Clothed in light e'r worlds could be,

Robed in mortal flesh is dying,
Crucified by sin for me.

O, mysterious condescending,
O, abandonment sublime,
Very God Himself is bearing
All the sufferings of time.

Let us not say that God is so transcendent, so majestic, so outside everything that He cannot suffer, and doesn't suffer. Love and impassibility are mutually exclusive. If God is love He suffers. If He doesn't suffer He isn't love. If incarnate Deity didn't suffer on Calvary's cross there is no Atonement for human sin.

Charles Wesley asked the question: 'O Love Divine! what hast Thou done?' He answers:

The immortal God hath died for me!

The Father's co-eternal Son

Bore all my sins upon the tree.

In another hymn Wesley declared:

'Tis mystery all, The Immortal dies!

Some may say that this is not theological. God cannot die. Well, it all depends on what is meant by 'dies'. Christ, the God-man Redeemer, tasted death for every man. The poet was trying to express the inexpressible. The truth is:

The transcendent God descended to a cross on Golgotha's brow. The ineffable God suffered for the world of sinful and sinning humanity. The God of love atoned for human sin in its dreadful totality. The God of grace and of power triumphed in the darkness of seeming defeat. This is the unchanging truth of the New Testament. The message of the Atonement is: 'To God's kind wisdom sinning souls, amid their sins, are dear'. Yes, all sinning souls amid their sins are loved by God. We look at some people in the world today, marred and broken by sin, and we wonder can God love them. It is a contradiction of the Gospel of the New Testament to say that God loves some, because of some merit in them, because they didn't sin in the way that others have sinned.

God has a heart big enough to take in the world of lost humanity. We have a Gospel for every man in all the world, no matter how sinful he may be.

Chapter 4

THE TRUTH ABOUT SALVATION

One fears that in these days when there is so much talk about the Church, and Church unity, there isn't enough said about Christ and salvation in Him. Salvation is a great Bible word, and we haven't yet begun to understand its full meaning. It means more than deliverance from sin's penalty and sin's power; it means wholeness, completeness, all-round well-being. One scholar says that salvation is being safe from the horrible long-term consequences of sin, and safe in the presence of God's utter holiness. It includes the whole of Christ's redemptive work in the believing soul, beginning with justification, being declared free from the penalty of the broken law and being received into fellowship with God; it continues with sanctification, being conformed into the likeness of Christ which is God's purpose in redemption; and it ends with glorification, being free from all sin and being like Christ, God's ideal.

Ephesians 1:13 says: 'In whom ye also trusted, after that ye heard the word of truth, the gospel of your salvation: in whom also after that ye believed, ye were sealed with that holy Spirit of promise'. All this is very simple and clear. We shouldn't allow anyone to complicate it. Notice: (i) They heard the Gospel message, the good news of salvation in Christ, (ii) They trusted in the Christ of the Gospel, the atoning, risen, reigning, redeeming, conquering Christ, (iii) Upon their believing in Christ they were sealed with the Holy Spirit as God's own possession. The gift of the Spirit to them, the moment they believed in Christ, was the Divine mark that they were Christians. This verse contradicts a whole lot of teaching in professedly Christian circles today.

Salvation is Man's Most Pressing Need

Notwithstanding all his amazing achievements, man is a sinner in the sight of God. He is under the judgement of God because of sin. He is unable to save himself, unable to meet the high demands of Divine righteousness. The Bible says: 'All have sinned, and come short of the glory of God' (Rom. 3:23). It says: 'Sin is the transgression of the law' (1 John 3:4). Sin is doing what God has commanded us not to do, and failing to do what He has commanded us to do. There are sins of commission and sins of omission.

The good news of the Gospel is that God in Christ has atoned for human sin, and provided salvation full and free for all men. There is deliverance from sin's power and penalty for all who believe in Christ as their Saviour. There is cleansing in the blood of Christ from the defilement of sin. This means the spiritual application of the finished work of Christ by the Holy Spirit in response to faith. This cleansing is something transcendently spiritual.

Salvation is the Gift of God

It is not the achievement of man. It cannot be earned; it must be taken as a free gift. 'The gift of God is eternal life through Jesus Christ our Lord' (Rom. 6:23). A gift is offered by one person to another person; it may be accepted or it may be refused. Salvation is the offer of God, in His sovereign grace and mercy, to sinful man who deserves nothing but His judgement because of his sin. It has to be freely accepted. There is no compulsion. Man isn't treated like a machine, but as a free moral being. Religion, to be of any moral and spiritual value must be free. Since salvation is the free gift of God it follows that we haven't to pay for it, or pray for it, or do the best we can for it; we take it as God's unmerited gift.

Dr Thomas Chalmers said: 'I must say that I never have had so close and satisfactory a view of the Gospel of salvation, as when I have been led to contemplate it in the light of a simple offer on the one side, and a simple acceptance on the other'.

Salvation is by Grace through Faith

It is not by sovereign grace without personal trust in the Lord Jesus Christ; and it is not by belief without the grace of God. Grace is the *procuring cause*; faith is the *appropriating cause*. Our Lord began His ministry by saying: 'Repent ye, and believe the Gospel' (Mark 1:15). Think again, change your mind, and believe the good news of forgiveness for you in Christ. If a man is so dead in sin that he cannot do anything, if he is just a lump of corruption and not a free moral being, our Lord would not have commanded him to repent and believe the Gospel. 'God commands all men everywhere to repent' (Acts 17:30). This is as universal as language can make it.

Ephesians 2;8 says: 'For by grace are ye saved through faith; and that not of yourselves: it is the gift of God'. The Amplified New Testament reads: 'For it is by free grace (God's unmerited favour) that you are saved (delivered from judgement and made partakers of Christ's salvation) through (your) faith. And this (salvation) is not of yourselves — of your own doing, it came not through your own striving — but it is the gift of God'.

Dr A.T. Robertson, the Greek expert, has a fine piece of scientific exegesis on this verse which is greatly needed today. He says: 'Grace is God's part, faith ours. And that (*Kai touto*) neuter, not feminine, *taute*, and so refers not to *pistis* (feminine), faith, or to *charis* (feminine also), grace but to the act of being saved by grace, conditioned on faith on our part. Paul shows that salvation does not have its source (*ex humen*, out of you) in men, but from God. Besides, it is God's gift (*doron*) and not the result of our work' (*Word Pictures in the New Testament*).

On Ephesians 2:8 John Calvin comments: 'When, on the part of man, the act of receiving salvation is made to consist in faith alone, all other means on which men are accustomed to rely, are discarded. Faith, then, brings a man empty to God, that he may be filled with the blessings of Christ, and so he adds, *not of yourselves*; that, claiming nothing for themselves, they may acknowledge God alone as the author of their salvation'. There is, then, man's act of receiving by faith the salvation that God in grace has provided. God's gift is not forced on anyone against his free choice. Man acknowledges that God is the sole author of salvation. In his bankruptcy *he comes* in faith to Christ for the supply of his every need. *He is not dragged* to Christ, like an object without a will. On the words, 'not of works' in Ephesians 2:9 John Calvin writes: 'Instead of what he had said, that their salvation is of grace, he now affirms, that it is the gift of God'. He continues: 'He says that the righteousness comes to us from the mercy of God alone, — is offered to us in Christ by the gospel, — and is received by faith alone, without the merit of works'. It is offered to us in Christ, and it has to be accepted. On Ephesians 2:8 Calvin says: 'And here we must advert to a very common error in the interpretation of this passage. Many persons restrict the word *gift* to faith alone. But Paul is only repeating in other words the former sentiment. His meaning is, "*not* that faith is the gift of God, but that salvation is given to us by God, or, that we obtain it by the gift of God". Before man is saved by the grace of God he must take what God offers'.

Reverend William Pringle, who translated Calvin's *Commentaries* from the original Latin, has a footnote on the words, 'that not of yourselves' in Ephesians 2:8 which says: 'It has been not a little debated, among both ancient and modern commentators, to what noun *touto* (that) should be referred. Some say, to *pisteos* (faith); others, to *chariti* (grace); though, on the sense of *pistis*, they differ in their view. The reference seems, however, to be neither to the one nor to the other, but to the subject of the foregoing *clause*, salvation by grace, through faith in Christ and his gospel; a view, I find, adopted by Dr Chandler, Dean Tucker, Dr McKnight, and Dr A. Clarke. And to show that this interpretation is not a mere novelty, I need only refer the reader to Theophylact who thus explains, "He does not say that faith is the gift of God; but to be saved by faith, this is the gift of God"'. The R.S.V. rendering of Ephesians 2:8 is: 'And this is not your own doing, it is the gift of God'. Sometimes theology is based on erroneous exegesis.

According to the New Testament it is the sovereign purpose of God to save those who believe in Christ. If a man is unsaved it is not because God is unwilling to save him; it is because he is unwilling to be saved. He will not trust in Christ. Hebrews 4:2 says: 'For unto us was the gospel preached, as well as unto them; but the word preached did not profit them, not being mixed with faith in them that heard it'. They heard the good news, but they didn't believe it, and, therefore, they weren't saved. Dr F.F. Bruce says: 'The practical implication is clear: it is not the hearing of the gospel, by itself, that brings salvation, but its appropriation by faith; and if that faith is a genuine faith, it will be a persistent faith' (*The Epistle to the Hebrews*). Paul said: 'It pleased God by the foolishness of preaching to save them that believe' (1 Cor. 1:21). There must be faith by those who hear the good news. It is not by foolish preaching, or by the foolishness of preaching, but by the Redeeming Message of the Cross, reckoned foolish and silly by the wise of this world, that God saves. The verb translated 'believe' in the New Testament means to cleave to, to trust in, to depend upon. Faith unto salvation is absolute reliance upon the Lord Jesus Christ and His finished work. It is not just an intellectual assent to theological propositions about Christ; it is heart trust in Him as personal Saviour and Lord. Dr James Denney said: 'Faith is man's absolute committal of himself for ever to the sin-bearing love of God for salvation' (*The Christian Doctrine of Reconciliation* p. 291).

In a paper entitled 'The Baptist Doctrine of the Church and Ecumenicity', W.H. Porter says: 'Almost universal among Baptists is the conviction that

Christian faith in a *personal voluntary commitment* of one's self to Jesus Christ as Lord and Saviour; and that the Church is a gathered fellowship of persons who have made such a commitment to Christ'.

Dr J. Gresham Machen says: 'The means which the Spirit of God uses in making men Christians, is faith; and faith is the response of the human soul to the gospel message. A man becomes convicted of sin; he sees himself as God sees him; he is in despair. And then the Lord Jesus is offered to him in the gospel — in the good news, that the guilt of sin has been blotted out by the wonderful sacrifice, which God Himself provided, in His mysterious love for sinners, on Calvary. The acceptance of that message is faith, faith in the Lord Jesus Christ; through faith a man becomes a child of God; and then follows a new life, with a victorious battle against sin' (*What is Christianity* p. 760).

Note, this scholar says, 'faith is the response of the human soul to the gospel message'. Unlike any other part of God's creation, man, under the ministry of the Holy Spirit, can make this response, which must be free and uncoerced to be of any spiritual value. Without this free, personal response to the Gospel message there can be no experience of God's saving grace. Many believe in other remedies for sin, than Christ and His finished work. They have faith, but it is in the wrong object. It is not the quantity of faith or the quality of faith, but the *object* of faith that matters. Little faith in a great Saviour, the Lord Jesus Christ, Who died and rose again, brings salvation. Great faith in ourselves, in our own good works, in the Church, in Sacraments, in anything else, is of no avail. Paul said: 'For I know Whom I have believed' (2 Tim. 1:12). To put it very simply, our all must be on Christ

assert "where necessity is, there can be no crown (as the reward of free choice)"' (*The Grace of God* p. 36).

John Oman says that the normal person is self-determined, and a moral person is self-determined according to his own self-direction. Oman says that Augustine declared for the freedom of the will, and Calvin for necessity. 'No one', says Oman, 'proves more conclusively than Calvin the utter hopelessness of ascribing everything to God, either directly, or through the operation of the universe, and yet holding man responsible for his doings' (*Grace and Personality* p. 48). Obviously, if man is not responsible for what he does, if he is driven by some external force that he cannot control, he cannot be judged at last, by God, for what he does. The Bible says: '*And they were judged every man according to their works*' (Rev. 20:13).

It is a repudiation of human responsibility, and a denial of human personality, for anyone to say, 'If God has decreed that I should be saved, I'll be saved; if He has decreed that I should be damned I'll be damned'. Man has a choice in his salvation. Otherwise, he is only a cog in the vast machine of predeterminism. Some are in danger of so emphasizing the truth of salvation *by grace alone* that they cut out personal faith. The New Testament says it is *by* grace *through* faith. It is *by grace alone* in its provision; but the provision, offered by God, must be taken by man.

In the New Testament the doctrine of justification by faith *alone* is as clear as crystal. Two verses, out of many, may be quoted. 'Knowing that a man is not justified by the works of the law, but by the faith of Jesus Christ, even we have believed in Jesus Christ, that we might be justified by the faith of Christ, and not by the works of the law: for by the works of the law shall no flesh be justified' (Gal. 2:16). 'The faith of Jesus Christ' means, faith in Jesus Christ. The Amplified New Testament rendering is very clear: 'Yet we know that a man is justified or reckoned righteous and in right standing with God, not by works of law but (only) through faith and (absolute) reliance on, and adherence to, and trust in Jesus Christ, the Messiah, the Anointed One'.

Galatians 3:11 says: 'But that no man is justified by the law in the sight of God is evident: for, the just shall live by faith'. These are not isolated texts taken out of their context. They express the whole teaching of the Bible.

James asks: 'Can faith save him?' (2:14). 'Can that faith save him?' (R.V.). A man's professed faith, without a new life of good works, is not a living faith in the living Christ. Paul is against the teaching that the works of the law are the means of justification. James is for the teaching that there must be the works of faith, works inspired by faith, as the evidence of salvation. We are justified by faith *alone*, but not by the faith that is alone.

Justification is more than the forgiveness of sins, wonderful though that is. It means that the past is blotted out and that we are declared free from the penalty of the broken law, also we are received into fellowship with God. It would be difficult to find a more adequate definition of justification, than that given by Dr A.H. Strong. He says: 'By justification we mean that judicial act of God by which, on account of Christ, to Whom the sinner is united by faith, He declares that sinner to be no longer exposed to the penalty of the law, but to be restored to His favour . . . .

J

Justification is the reversal of God's attitude toward the sinner, because of the sinner's new relation to Christ. God did condemn; He now acquits. He did repel; He now admits to favour' (*Systematic Theology* p. 849).

It has been said that Shakespeare knew human nature. He bears witness to his own need of atonement for sin. In his last Will and Testament he writes: 'First, I commend my soul into the hands of God, my Creator, hoping and assuredly believing, through the only merits of Jesus Christ my Saviour, to be made partaker of life everlasting'. He calls Christ, 'The world's ransom, blessed Mary's Son' (Richard II 4:1). He speaks of the death of Christ as 'the death of Him who died for all'. It is not because people know too much that they reject Christ; it is because they don't know enough. True knowledge, humbles people, and leads to Him who was Truth Incarnate.

Salvation has been Provided by God for all Men

Here are words sublime in their simplicity: 'For the grace of God hath appeared bringing salvation to all men' (Titus 2:11). Dr F.F. Bruce has this rendering: 'The grace of God has shone upon us, bringing salvation for all mankind'. Dr Guthrie says: '*To all men* should therefore naturally belong to the noun (as R.V.), showing the universal scope of Christian salvation' (*The Pastoral Epistles*). To take 'all men' as meaning, 'All classes of men, even slaves and kings' is just exactly what the verse does *not* say. It says *all men*. The offer of salvation to all men, and the acceptance of it, are two totally different things. God's salvation has been provided for all men, it is offered to all men as a free gift: but not all will accept it, therefore, not all will be saved. Archbishop Trench said: 'Every man is Lord of the house of his own heart: it is his fortress: he must open the gates of it. He has the mournful prerogative and privilege of refusing to open'. If man refuses to open the door from the inside, God Almighty will not prize it open against his will.

Dr Newport White says: 'The justification of this insistence on the universal necessity for right conduct is the all-embracing scope of the saving grace of God, which has visibly appeared as a call to repentance, a help to amendment of life, and a stimulus to hope . . . . No rank or class or type of mankind is outside the saving experience of God's grace' (*Expositor's Greek Testament*). By their own deliberate choice men put themselves outside. They may reject God's provision for them in Christ.

Luke says: 'But the Pharisees and the lawyers rejected the counsel of God against themselves, being not baptized of him' (7:30). The word rendered 'counsel' (*Boule*) means purpose, deliberate intention, 'especially the purpose of God respecting the salvation of men through Christ' (*Thayer*). It was God's will and purpose, that they should have obeyed His command through John, and repented of sin and got themselves baptized, but they rejected this, and missed God's blessing. Dr A.T. Robertson's comment on this verse is: 'These legalistic interpreters of the law refused to admit the need of confession of sin on their part, and so set aside the baptism of John. They annulled God's purposes of grace so far as they applied to them' (*Word Pictures in the New Testament*). It is clear, then, that man can annul the purpose of God to bless him. God wants to save and bless men but they oppose Him and reject His will. He doesn't force His blessings on them. Norval Geldenhuys was a scholar without any

Arminian tendencies. On Luke 7:30, he says: 'To their own undoing, they made His plan of redemption worthless, so far as they themselves were concerned' (*The Gospel of Luke*). He says that we are here face to face with the paradox of Divine Sovereignty, and human responsibility — a paradox which no human mind can ever solve. Dr Plummer remarks: 'Free will enables each man to annul God's purpose for his salvation'. If this is not so, then we are forced to the conclusion that it is God's will not to save those who are not saved. This would be against the whole tenor of Bible revelation.

The Lord Jesus said: 'Strive to enter in at the strait gate: for many, I say unto you, will seek to enter in, and shall not be able' (Luke 13:24). He means: 'Keep on striving to enter', or, 'Strain every nerve'. Plummer says: 'The door leads directly into the house, and is so narrow that only those who are thoroughly in earnest can pass through it . . . . Jesus does not say that there are many who strive in vain to enter, but that there *will* be many who *will seek* in vain to enter, *after the time of salvation is past*. Those who continue to strive now, succeed' (*The International Critical Commentary* St. Luke, p. 346). Geldenhuys says: 'They are not to waste their time and strength in arguments as to how many will be saved, but every one must strive hard, and make sure that he himself is saved, for, whether the saved are to be many or few, one thing is certain — the gate leading to life is strait, and only those who strive with might and main, and wholeheartedly enter, will be saved'. The Lord Jesus is not teaching salvation by struggling, by doing the best we can. Salvation is by accepting God's gift. But many things will seek to keep us from accepting this inestimable gift. The devil himself will do his best to keep us from Christ. We must fight against anything, and anyone, that would keep us from entering into the blessing of salvation in Christ. Some give up the struggle against the enemy, and miss God's salvation. They allow self-interest, friends, wealth, the world, the opinions of men, to win the victory, to keep them from Christ. One must say that if everything is predetermined by God beforehand, and man has no choice in his salvation, the words of our Lord to strive to enter, are meaningless. Indeed, they are altogether out of place.

In Luke 14:23,24, we read: 'And the Lord said unto the servant Go out into the highways and hedges, and compel them to come in, that my house may be filled. For I say unto you, that none of those men which were bidden shall taste of my supper'. A.T. Robertson says: 'By persuasion of course. There is no thought of compulsory salvation'. 'Not to use force, but to constrain them against the reluctance which such poor creatures would feel, at accepting the invitation of a great Lord' (Vincent). Plummer points out that a single servant could not use force, and those who refused were not dragged in. He says that the text gives no sanction to religious persecution. 'By showing that physical force was not used, it rather condemns it'.

Geldenhuys writes: 'By their foolish action they have finally excluded themselves. When those people who have rejected the invitation of God, extended to them by Him in Christ, try to seek admission to His kingdom, at the end-time, when it will be revealed in full glory, it will be utterly refused to them — because they have allowed the time of grace to pass by, they have themselves to blame for their exclusion . . . . He who refuses to accept the invitation, will, through his own fault, have no share in the rich blessings in the everlasting kingdom of God'. This is against some theological systems, but it is the teaching of Christ. 'Jesus does not here teach, either a mechanically operating predestination, which determines from all eternity who shall, or shall not, be brought into the kingdom. Neither does He proclaim that man's entry into the kingdom is purely his own affair. The two essential points in His teaching are that no man can enter the kingdom without the invitation of God, and that no man can remain outside it but by his own deliberate choice. Man cannot save himself; but he can damn himself. And it is this latter fact that makes the preaching of Jesus so urgent. For he sees the deepest tragedy of human life, not in the many wrong and foolish things that men do, or the many good and wise things that they fail to accomplish, but in their rejection of God's greatest gift' (T.W. Manson, op. cit., p. 422).

Romans 9:22 says that God 'endured with much long-suffering the vessels of wrath, fitted to destruction'. It should be noted carefully that Paul does not say that God prepared them for destruction. That the people themselves are responsible, is clear from the rest of the Bible. They prepared themselves for destruction. Dr Charles Hodge says that the word 'fitted' in Romans 9:22 admits of being taken as in the Middle Voice, and may be rendered, 'who have fitted themselves for destruction'. He says: 'Wicked men are prepared for destruction by God, not as being created for that purpose, but as being devoted to it on account of their sins, and borne with, until they are ripe for their doom' (*Commentary on Romans* p. 286). Sanday and Headlam say that 'vessels of wrath' in Romans

9:22 means 'vessels which deserve God's wrath'. They deserve it because of their deliberate, persistent rebellion against the will of God for them. Paul says most explicitly that God showed great long-suffering with them. He, therefore, desired their salvation, not their damnation. He didn't, in some arbitrary way, prepare them for destruction.

On Romans 9, Dr James Denney says: 'It would not be right to say that Paul here refers the eternal salvation, or perdition, of individuals to an absolute decree of God which has no relation to what they are, or do, but rests simply on His inscrutable will' (*Expositor's Greek Testament* vol. 2, p. 661). On verse 22, Denney says: 'It is not long-suffering if the end in view is a more awful display of wrath; there is no real long-suffering unless the end in view is to give the sinner *place for repentance*'. On Romans 9:23 Denney says: 'The text presents no ground whatever for importing into it the idea of an unconditional eternal decree'. In the New Testament it is clear beyond all cavil, that salvation is conditional on man repenting and believing, changing his mind and putting his trust in Christ. You cannot have unconditional election, and conditional salvation. They are mutually exclusive. It is true that God takes the initiative, but man is left free to respond or rebel, respond and be saved, or rebel and be lost. God *calls* men from among the Gentiles and from among the Jews, but He doesn't *drag* them to Himself without their free consent. Dr William Barclay says: 'God cannot do anything which contradicts His own nature. God cannot be responsible for any act which is unjust and which, in fact, breaks His own laws. We find it hard, and even impossible, to conceive of a God who irresponsibly gives mercy to one, and not to another' (*The Letter to the Romans* p. 138). God has the indisputable right to be Absolute Sovereign, because He is a God of wisdom, of love, and of justice. But we must never conclude that He acts in a way which is contrary to His love and His justice.

Paul uses the figure of God as the potter, and man as the clay, but the Bible teaches clearly that there is a fundamental difference between a human person, and a lump of clay. The clay hasn't personality, that is, self-consciousness and self-determination; it hasn't emotions, volition, conscience, mind, spirit; it hasn't to make decisions; it cannot feel or know; it is not commanded to repent and believe in Christ; it cannot talk back; it is not judged at last for not responding to the appeal of the Gospel. 'It is a basic fact of the Gospel' says Dr Barclay, 'that God does not treat men as a potter treats a lump of clay; He treats them as a loving father treats his child' (*The Letter to the Romans* p. 140).

Of old God said: 'But ye are they that forsake the Lord . . . . Therefore will I number you to the sword, and ye shall all bow down to the slaughter: because when I called, ye did not answer; when I spake, ye did not hear; but did evil before mine eyes, and did choose that wherein I delighted not' (Isa. 65:11,12). It is evident that God didn't force them to do what He wanted them to do. Our Lord said: 'I would; ye would not' (Luke 13:34). Quite definitely Christ taught His own willingness and man's deliberate, persistent unwillingness. He didn't force Himself upon the people.

Man is responsible for what he does with the gift of God in Christ. By what he does with it he determines his own eternal destiny.

On Luke 14:23, '*Compel* them to come in', John Calvin says: 'I do not disapprove of the use which Augustine frequently made of this passage against the Donatists, to prove that godly princes may lawfully issue edicts, for *compelling* obstinate and rebellious persons, to worship the true God, and to maintain the unity of the faith'. We are bound to say that worship that is compelled by the edicts of men, and not impelled by the love of God, is not worship at all; it is dead formality without any real spiritual meaning. 'Compel' in Luke 14:23 should be 'constrain'. The word is used, not in the sense of external compulsion, but in the sense of moral and logical constraint. Jesus constrained His disciples to get into a ship (Matt. 14:22). He didn't drag them in, against their will. People are drawn to Christ by His love and by His Spirit, but they are not dragged into the kingdom against their free choice.

John Oman says: 'The long sorrowful experience of the ages seems to show that the last thing God thinks of doing, is to drive mankind, with resistless rein, on the highway of righteousness' (*Grace and Personality* p. 26). Man, as a moral personality, is left free to make even a fatal choice.

General Booth used to say: 'Friends, Jesus shed His blood to pay the price, and He bought from God enough salvation to go round'. The super-intellectuals will reject this as crude. Certain theologians will be unable to fit it into their theological system. This writer, with the New Testament in his hand, is compelled to say: 'Yes, glory to God, yes; there is enough salvation in Christ and His atoning work, for everyone who will come and take it'. If every man in all the world accepted it there would still be enough for millions of new worlds yet unborn. On the words of General Booth, Bishop Gailor said: 'I feel that his view of salvation is different from mine. Yet such teaching, partial as it is, lifts men by the thousands from the mire and vice of sin, into the power and purity of a new life in Jesus Christ'. The Gospel is God's saving dynamic to everyone that believeth, but not to him who rejects it.

Salvation is through Faith in Christ without Water Baptism

A few verses of Scripture must suffice. The Lord Jesus said to the sick of the palsy: 'Son thy sins be forgiven thee' (Mark 2:5 A.V.). 'My son, your sins are forgiven' (R.S.V.). There is nothing here about water baptism. This comes after salvation. Our Lord claimed the right to forgive sins, so He claimed equality with God, for only God can forgive sins. The Apostle Peter said: 'To Him (the Lord Jesus) give all the prophets witness, that through his name whosoever believeth in him shall receive remission of sins' (Acts 10:43). There is nothing here about baptism being essential to the forgiveness of sins. If it were, Peter would not have omitted it on this very important occasion. Pardon, through faith in Christ, is an essential prerequisite to baptism. The Apostle Paul said: 'Be it known unto you therefore, men and brethren, that through this man (the God-man) is preached unto you the forgiveness of sins; And by him all that believe are justified from all things, from which ye could not be justified by the law of Moses' (Acts 13:38,39). 'Believe on the Lord Jesus Christ, and

thou shalt be saved, and thy house' (Acts 16:31).
Where there was household salvation, and household
baptism, there was first of all household faith.
Everyone in the house believed unto salvation.

Some teach that water baptism is essential to the
forgiveness of sins. They base their theory on the
words, 'for the remission of sins' (Mark 1:4; Acts 2:38).
It should be noted that, in English, 'for' is sometimes
used in the sense of, 'because of'. For instance, a man is
hanged *for* murder. He isn't hanged in order that he
may commit murder, but because he has committed it.
A man is fined *for* stealing. He isn't fined in order that
he may steal, but because he has stolen. Sometimes in
the New Testament the preposition translated 'for'
(*eis*) has the meaning of, 'because of'. In Matt. 3:11 we
read: 'I indeed baptise you with water unto
repentance'. 'Unto' translates *eis*. It is clear from John's
teaching that he didn't baptise people in order that
they might repent, change their minds, but because
they had repented. His first command was 'Repent'.
Our Lord said: 'They repented at the preaching of
Jonah' (Matt. 12:41). 'At' translates *eis*. Nobody would
ask us to believe that they repented in order that Jonah
might preach. The direct opposite is true. They
repented because Jonah preached. The preposition *eis*
is used in the sense of, 'because of'. On Mark 1:4, Dr
A.T. Robertson says: 'Certainly John did not mean
that the baptism was the means of obtaining the
forgiveness of their sins, or necessary to the remission
of sins. The trouble lies in the use of EIS which is
sometimes used when purpose is expressed, but
sometimes when there is no such idea. Possibly "with
reference to" is as good a translation as is possible'
(*Word Pictures in the New Testament*). Robertson

proves that sometimes in the New Testament *eis* is used when there is no idea of purpose. It is used in the sense of 'because of'.

There are three powerful arguments against the teaching that water baptism is essential to salvation, to the forgiveness of sins. (i) It is against our own experience. We know that we were saved, justified, regenerated, forgiven when we first trusted in Christ, and before we were baptized. We got ourselves baptized, because we knew we were pardoned through faith in the Redeemer's blood. (ii) It is against our observation. We know real believers in Christ, men and women who are saved and forgiven, and they are not yet baptized. (iii) It is against the great Bible doctrine that the living Christ, and the trusting soul, are sufficient in the matter of personal salvation. The teaching that baptism is essential to the forgiveness of sins brings in a third party. A third person must baptize the man, for no one can baptize himself. It limits God to the act of man. It is in essence Romanism. We believe that God is sovereign and free, and can save the believer in Christ without the act of a third party, sinful and erring man.

Salvation and the Will of God

Paul wrote: 'For this is good and acceptable in the sight of God our Saviour; who will have all men to be saved, and to come unto the knowledge of the truth' (1 Tim. 2:3,4). We should be careful not to read into these words something that is not there; and we should not leave out something that has been put there by the Holy Spirit. The Apostle does not say that God decreed to save all men irrespective of their reaction to the message of the Gospel. The New Testament makes it clear that salvation, the forgiveness of sins, life in Christ, being right with God, is conditional. It is only those who believe in Christ, those who trust Him as their personal Saviour, who are saved, who are justified, who are regenerated. If God decreed to save all men, regardless of what they do when they hear the Gospel, then all would be saved. But God waits for man's free response to His appeal. Our Lord said: 'I would, ye would not' (Luke 13:34).

On 1 Timothy 2:4, John Calvin writes; 'He demonstrates that God has at heart the salvation of all, because he invites all to the acknowledgement of the truth'. If God has at heart the salvation of all, He cannot possibly have predestinated some of them to eternal damnation without giving them an offer of salvation.

The force of the verb rendered 'willeth' in 1 Timothy 2:4 is to will, to wish, implying volition and purpose. It expresses the determination to do a thing. W.E. Vine says: 'It signifies the gracious desire of God for all men to be saved; not all men are willing to accept His condition, depriving themselves either by self-established criterion of perverted reason, or because of their self-indulgent preference for sin' (*Expository Dictionary of New Testament Words*).

On 1 Timothy 2:4, Dr Ellicott remarks that all attempted restrictions of this vital text are as much to be reprehended on the one hand, as that perilous universalism on the other. The Scriptures declare in the most explicit terms that God loves all men in spite of their sin, so He desires the salvation of *all*. Dr Ellicott says: 'That some are indisputably not saved (Matt. 25:41; Rev. 20:10,15) is not due to any circumscription or inefficacy of the Divine will, but to man's rejection of the special means of salvation, which God has been pleased to appoint . . . . In a word, redemption is universal yet conditional; all may be saved, yet all will not be saved because all will not conform to God's appointed conditions' (*St. Paul's Epistles to Timothy and Titus*).

Dr James Denney held that a dogmatic universalism is unscriptural and unethical. He wrote: 'The very conception of human freedom involves the possibility of its permanent misuse, or of what our Lord Himself calls "eternal sin", Mark 2:29' (*Studies in Theology* p. 255). 'The very fact of human freedom demands the possibility of choosing that which is sin' (J.R. Taylor, *God Loves Like That!* p. 186).

Paul says in Ephesians 1:10, 'That in the dispensation of the fullness of times he might gather together in one all things in Christ, both which are in heaven, and which are on earth; even in Him'. Meyer believed that the true interpretation of this verse is that 'the allusion is not to the restoration of all *fallen individuals*, but to the restoration of universal *harmony*, implying that the wicked are to be excluded from the kingdom of God'. Dr A.H. Strong held that Christ, the immanent God, is already in this world present with every human soul, quickening the conscience, giving to each man his opportunity, and making every decision between right and wrong, a true probation. 'In choosing evil against their better judgement', he says, 'even the heathen reject Christ'. (*Systematic Theology* p. 1040). Endless persistence in sin, eternal rebellion against the will of God, is not only a terrible possibility, but, according to the Scriptures, it is an awful fact.

Acts 3:20,21, says: 'And he shall send Jesus Christ,

which before was preached unto you: Whom the heavens must receive until the times of restoration of all things, which God hath spoken by the mouth of all his holy prophets since the world began'. The word rendered 'restoration', *apokatastasis*, is used in the papyri of the repair of a public way, the restoration of estates to their rightful owners, the balancing of accounts. As a technical medical term, it means complete restoration to health. In Acts 3:21, according to Dr F.F. Bruce, it may be rendered 'establishment' or 'fulfilment', 'referring', he says, 'to the fulfilment of all Old Testament prophecy, culminating in the establishment of God's kingdom on earth' (*The Acts of the Apostles* p. 112). On the word *apokatastasis*, Dr Plumptre says: 'It does not necessarily involve, as some have thought, the final salvation of all men, but it does express the idea of a state in which "righteousness", and not "sin" shall have dominion over a redeemed and new-created world'. The sin and rebellion of man shall have no place in God's perfect Kingdom. They shall be confined to the place prepared for them. 'How this restoration of all things was to be effected, and what was involved in it, St. Peter does not say, but his whole trend of thought shows that it was made dependent upon man's repentance, upon his heart being right with God' (*Expositor's Greek Testament*). There is yet to be a new heaven and a new earth, which will be ushered in, not by the efforts of man, but by the return of the God-man in power and in glory.

Professor E.Y. Mullins says that in Philippians 2:9-11; Ephesians 1:10; and Colossians 1:20 the reference is to 'the universe as a whole rather than to individuals . . . . In Philippians Christ is declared to be universal Lord . . . . He will have no rival in authority and power . . . . In Ephesians He is represented as the unifying bond of all things. God brings to a head or recapitulates all things in Him. The parts of the universe are conceived of as scattered. He reunites them. All things are thus summed up, or headed up, in Him' (*The Christian Religion in Its Doctrinal Expression* p. 497). In answer to those who argue that God is love, and love can never rest content while any are lost, this scholar replies: 'We must not overlook the uniform representations of the New Testament that an element in the problem is always man's attitude to the gracious appeal of God . . . . The outcome of His love in relation to men is conditioned by their attitude toward that love. He deals with us as moral beings, responsible and free' (*The Christian Religion in Its Doctrinal Expression* p. 499). Dr Mullins affirms that there is a retributive element in punishment, but assuming that there is also a corrective element, it does not follow that it will always prove efficacious. He continues: 'Sinners continue in sin in the life to come, punishment simply keeps pace with sin. If the sin should cease, the punishment would cease. Eternal punishment for the incorrigibly sinful, therefore, follows not from the fact of a finite earthy sin, but from the endless or immortal existence of the sinner' (*The Christian Religion in Its Doctrinal Expression* p. 500).

In Salvation there is the Divine side and there is the human side
    God draws graciously, but He never drags violently. Man is not a puppet on a string. He is a free moral being with powers of choice. No one is shut out of the kingdom of God, if he really wants to come in. No one

is dragged in, if he prefers to stay out. Our Lord said: 'No man can come to me, except the Father which hath sent me draw him' (John 6:44). The initiative is always God's, sovereign and persistent: but the response is man's, free and uncoerced. In John 6:44, it is the Greek word *helkuo* that is used, not *suro*. *Suro* means to drag, to haul. It is used of a net, 'dragging the net with fishes' (John 21:8). It is used of violently dragging people along, 'haling men and women' (Acts 8:3), 'dragging off men and women' (R.S.V.). Archbishop Trench says that in the word *suro* there is always the notion of force, but in *helkuo* this notion is not necessarily present. 'This less violent significance, usually present in *helkuo*, but always absent from *suro*, is seen in the metaphorical use of *helkuo*, to signify drawing by inward power, by Divine impulse, John 6:44; 12:32' (W.E. Vine). If *suro* has been used in these verses we would have had our Lord's authority for believing in irresistible force.

In answer to those who give the verb 'to be saved' in 1 Timothy 2:4, a weaker sense of 'preserve' or 'protect', Dr Guthrie replies: 'But the passage as a whole seems too theological to be taken in this sense, and the concluding part of the verse, *to come unto the knowledge of the truth*, accords better with spiritual salvation than natural preservation' (*The Pastoral Epistles*). It is absurd to suggest that God wills to preserve or protect all men, but He is unwilling to save some of them. He doesn't preserve men in order to damn them, without their having a fair chance to be saved. Men damn themselves by rejecting Christ and refusing salvation in Him. No one will be lost for ever because God didn't make any provision for him, but because he didn't appropriate what God, in marvellous

K

love, and boundless grace, provided for him.

Peter tells us that God 'is long suffering to usward, not willing that any should perish, but that all should come to repentance' (2 Pet. 3:9).

Paul says: 'We trust in the living God, who is the Saviour of all men, specially of those that believe' (1 Tim. 4:10). 'While God is potentially the Saviour of all, He is actually Saviour of the *pistoi*' (believers) (White). Saviour means preserver, but as E.K. Simpson points out 'Christianity raises the word to a higher plain'. Difficult texts of Scripture must not be interpreted in such a way as to contradict clear declarations of the inspired Word which don't need any interpretation by man. The theory that some men are predestinated by God to eternal damnation, without getting any offer of salvation through faith in Christ, stands condemned at the bar of Bible revelation. It is the most God-dishonouring dogma ever fabricated by the distorted mind of man.

Luke says: 'And as many as were ordained to eternal life believed' (Luke 13:48). Dr R.K. Knowling writes: 'There is no countenance here for the *absolutum decretum* of the Calvinists, since verse 46 had already shown that the Jews had acted through their own choice' (*The Expositor's Greek Testament*). Some take the verb as middle, not passive, 'As many as had set themselves for eternal life believed'. In support of this, Rendall refers to 1 Corinthians 16:15; 'They addicted themselves to the ministry of the saints'. They gave themselves gladly and freely to the service of God's people. They weren't conscripted into service against their free choice.

Living Gospels, has this rendering of Acts 13:48; 'And as many as wanted eternal life, believed'. This fits well into the context of the words. The Jews heard the Gospel. Paul said to them: 'But seeing ye put it from you, and judge yourselves unworthy of eternal life, lo, we turn to the Gentiles' (v.46). He didn't say to the Jews: 'You are elected to damnation, therefore, we leave you. The Gentiles are elected to eternal salvation, therefore, we go to them'. The record is that the Gentiles 'were glad, and glorified the word of the Lord' (v.48). They rejoiced in the message of salvation proclaimed by Paul, believed it, and were saved. The message of the Gospel must be believed, if salvation is to be experienced. No one who is really saved will ever be lost. He who really believed in Christ at the beginning, and so was born again of the Holy Spirit, will keep on believing and is eternally secure. He who does not keep on believing really didn't believe in Christ unto salvation at the beginning, and so will be lost for ever. It is not true that a man can be truly saved today, and be eternally lost tomorrow. It is true that a man may *appear* to be saved today, may *profess* to be saved today, and be eternally lost tomorrow. No member of the Body of Christ, the true Church, will be lost.

A Warning Note

Eternal issues are at stake. Man determines his own eternal destiny by his reaction to God's appeal in the Gospel. Every man is free to vote. He may vote himself into the mansions of eternal glory, or into the confines of eternal destruction.

Men and women are not taken to heaven, and sent to hell, in an arbitrary way. Dr Shedd said: 'Eternal punishment supposes the freedom of the human will, and is impossible without it. Self-determination runs parallel with hell' (*Dogmatic Theology* 2 p. 715). Shedd was not an Arminian.

Dr E.Y. Mullins says: 'Hell is the monumental expression of the abuse of human freedom'. No one is cast into hell in an arbitrary kind of way. Men and women go there of their own free choice. Judas went to his own place, the place he prepared for himself, and the place he prepared himself for.

Here is a solemn word for those who obey not the Gospel: 'And to you who are troubled rest with us, when the Lord Jesus shall be revealed from heaven with His mighty angels, in flaming fire, taking vengeance on them that know not God, and that obey not the gospel of our Lord Jesus Christ: Who shall be punished with everlasting destruction from the presence of the Lord, and from the glory of his power' (2 Thess. 1:7-9). The Revised Standard Version Margin has: 'Eternal destruction, not annihilation but endless ruin in separation from Christ'. W.E. Vine says: 'The idea is not extinction, but ruin; loss, not of being, but of well-being' (*Expository Dictionary of New Testament Words*). The solemn note of the Gospel has to be sounded with compassion. Dr R.W. Dale said of D.L. Moody that he had the right to preach the Gospel because he could never speak of a lost soul without tears of Christly compassion in his eyes. Sometimes there is a hardness in the preaching of judgement that is repellent. We should remember that our Lord wept over the doomed city.

On our Lord's words of lamentation over Jerusalem, Dr Campbell Morgan says: 'There is a heart-break in them, the heart-break of God. There is in them the threnody of eternal pity'. One scholar and theologian says that it is not irreverent to believe that there may be in the heart of God something akin to broken-heartedness, at the refusal of Salvation by the sinner. He doesn't say that there is broken-heartedness, but something akin to it. Human language cannot adequately express the feelings of the heart of God. There is a hardline theology that is away from the heart of New Testament revelation — incarnate Deity suffering on Calvary's Cross for the salvation of lost men.

On God's judgement Dr James Denney said: 'We can trust the God and Father of our Lord Jesus Christ, that it will not fall on any who do not freely and deliberately pronounce it themselves'. We can rest on this: A God of unutterable love, of unerring wisdom, and of inflexible justice will do what is right. This is good news for us all.

The Appeal by the Gospel Preacher

Though we believe in the ministry of the Holy Spirit, without which there can be no salvation, we must urge people to obey the Gospel, to repent and believe in Christ. Great Biblical truths must be preached, not in a cold, calculating way, but with warm-hearted compassion, and with pressing urgency. God says: 'Look unto me, and be ye saved, all the ends of the earth: for I am God, and there is none else' (Isa. 45:22). We have the universality of the Divine appeal — '*all the ends of the earth*'. We have the simplicity of the Divine terms — '*LOOK*'. The youngest can look; the oldest can look; the weakest can look; the poorest can look; the down-and-out can look; the dying can look.

Through Isaiah 45:22, C.H. Spurgeon found salvation. The unlettered preacher, that snowy Sunday morning, said to young Spurgeon: 'Look to Jesus, look, look, look'. Spurgeon says: 'I did look and there, and then, the cloud was gone, the darkness had rolled away, and that moment I saw the sun. I could have risen on the instant and sung of the precious blood of Christ and of the simple faith that looks alone to Him. I looked until I could almost have looked my eyes away; and in heaven I will look still, in joy unutterable'. Yes, he had to look to Christ, and if he hadn't looked he wouldn't have been saved. Spurgeon closes one of his sermons with these words: 'I invite you, in my Master's name, to accept pardon through His blood'. Pardon is the gift of God, but it has to be accepted before it becomes ours. Spurgeon closes another sermon with these words: 'Hundreds of you are without God, and without Christ. And may I not plead with you? Is a gloomy religious system to hold me captive and never let me speak? . . . . God sends me as an ambassador now; but if ye listen not to me, He will not send an ambassador next time, but an execution-er'. Again he said: 'Thou art nothing. Wilt thou have Christ? Here He stands. Ask: it is all He wants'. You see, Spurgeon appealed to sinners to do something, to do what God commands them to do; to repent and believe in Christ as their Saviour and Lord. The theological hardliners of Spurgeon's day were against him because of his evangelistic appeal. It is true that no man can be saved without God. But it is also true that there is no man that God is unwilling to save, 'None need perish, For Christ hath died'.

A Redeeming Gospel with Social Implications

Though we do not preach the purely 'Social Gospel' advocated by some, we realize that the Evangelical

Gospel has social implications. In 1 John 3:17, there is a very practical word for all Christians. The Apostle says: 'If a man is rich and sees his brother in need, yet closes his heart against his brother, how can he claim that he has love for God in his heart?' (T.E.V.). 'Love for God', 'Objective genitive', says Dr David Smith, 'inspired by and answering to the love which God feels (subjective genitive)'. Helping the one in need is a proof of the indwelling love of God. One has the conviction that Evangelical Christians have failed here. They have not shown in a practical way, that the love of God is in their hearts. Dogmas in the mind can never take the place of love in the heart. God's love is unmerited; it is universal in its scope; it is self-giving; and it cannot be quenched by the waters of indifference, opposition, and self-seeking. Dr David Smith says: 'Love must be practical. It is easy to "lay down one's life": martyrdom is heroic and exhilarating; the difficulty lies in doing the little things, facing day by day the petty sacrifices, and self-denials, which no one notices and no one applauds' (*Expositor's Greek Testament* vol. 5, p.186). On 'shutteth up his bowels of compassion', Dr Smith says that the metaphor is locking the chamber of the heart instead of flinging it wide open, and lavishing its treasures.

Levi Palmer says that love becomes eyes to the blind, feet to the lame, and ears to the deaf. 'The poor, the hungry, and the wounded, soon know when love is in its holy temple, and they watch daily at its gates, waiting at the posts of its doors. If, then, we meet with a professor whose heart is unmoved by the cry of want, we may be sure that he is sounding brass and a clanging symbol . . . . It is quite easy to indulge ourselves in lofty ideals, which lie out of the way of everyday experience, and yet find it very hard to do the commonplace things which our hands find to do'. We should keep the balance between being sound in doctrine, and being practical in helping the needy. Believing and behaving should never be divorced. Some are all doctrine and no practice. Others are all practice and no doctrine. Both are extremes which the Bible condemns.

In 1966 H.F.R. Catherwood was appointed as Director-General of the National Economic Development Council. He has written a book entitled *The Christian in Industrial Society*. He says: 'The Christian should have no fear of stepping into the world of affairs. Men of faith have been there before him. Joseph was a ruler in Egypt. Daniel was a ruler both in Babylon and Persia . . . . Although the Apostles, as spiritual leaders, did not pronounce on secular politics, the Epistle of James is full of blistering social criticism'. James says: 'And now, you rich people, listen to me! Weep and wail over the miseries that are coming upon you! Your riches have rotted away, and your clothes have been eaten by moths. Your gold and silver are covered with rust, and this rust will be a witness against you, and eat up your flesh like fire. You have piled up riches in these last days. You have not paid the wages to the men who work in your fields. Hear their complaints! And the cries of those who gather in your crops, have reached the ears of God, the Lord Almighty. Your life here on earth has been full of luxury and pleasure. You have condemned and murdered the innocent man, and he does not resist you' (5:1-6, T.E.V.).

Commenting on James 5, one writer says truly: 'No

Marxist could exceed James's criticism of the evil rich — the exploiters and extortioners (3,4), the self-indulgent (5), and those who have used wealth to obtain, and misuse, power over others (6). This is a Christian view of wealth that the Church has not always been willing to teach'. It is the Godless rich who are in view. The Godless poor will not escape the judgement of God because of their poverty. They will not be saved because they are poor materially. Rich and poor expose themselves to the righteous judgement of God because of their rejection of Christ, and of salvation in Him. There is no sin in the possession of riches. It consists in the misuse of them, in making a god of them, the only god we know. Riches should be used to the glory of God and the good of others.

If there had been true New Testament Christianity in the world, there might never have been the rise and the spread of Communism. There is no point in debating about Vestments, Liturgy, and Dogma if men and women are in need all round us.

Amos has been called the prophet of doom. His message was one of Divine judgement coming upon the Godless rich and careless people of his days. He records God as saying: 'Seek good, and not evil, that ye may live: and so the Lord, the God of hosts, shall be with you, as ye have spoken. Hate the evil, and love the good, and establish judgement in the gate: it may be that the Lord God of hosts will be gracious unto the remnant of Joseph'. (5:14,15). Today Amos would be looked upon as rather tactless, not having the right approach. He said: 'Hear this word, ye kine of Bashan, that are in the mountain of Samaria, which oppresses the poor, which crush the needy' (4:1). He was addressing people, and likening them to the cows of Bashan. This was bound to come home to the hearts of his hearers. The richest pastureland of Israel lay in Bashan, and the cows there were fat and full. The prophet had seen them lying bulging with grass and thinking about nothing. He was saying: 'Ye lazy, over-fed, thoughtless, self-satisfied, earth-bound people, hear the word of the Lord'. The Bible is not against riches as such. It is against a selfish use of riches. It is against one man exploiting another man for personal gain. God says: 'But let judgement run down as waters, and righteousness as a mighty stream' (Amos 5:24). J.B. Phillips says: 'It should be remembered that these messages of denunciation (in Amos) were delivered in an atmosphere of unprecedented material prosperity, accompanied by a widespread decay of moral values, and a wicked oppression of the poor. Disaster seemed most unlikely, yet within a very few years four kings of Israel had been assassinated, then Hoshea was deposed and imprisoned, and Israel ceased to be a nation' (*Four Prophets* p. 3). There is Divine judgement as well as Divine salvation. Men expose themselves to the former by rejecting the latter. Being right with God, through faith in Christ, we do what is right amongst our fellow men.

The full-orbed Gospel of the New Testament is: God loves all men; Christ died for all men; salvation has been provided for all men; it is offered to all men as a free gift. Man is responsible for what he does with it. If anyone is lost for ever, it is his own fault. Paul was proud of the Gospel because he knew 'it is the power of God unto salvation to every one that believeth; to the

Jew first, and also to the Greek' (Rom. 1:16). No one can raise any objection to a Gospel like this, a Gospel that tells of a loving God, and a living Saviour, Who are seeking the highest good of every man, for Time and Eternity.